FOOTBALL
IS A FUNNY GAME

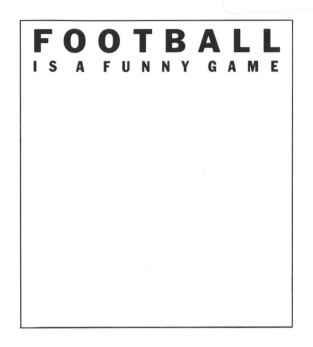

FOOTBALL
IS A FUNNY GAME
ACCORDING TO
SAINT & GREAVSIE

IAN ST JOHN & JIMMY GREAVES

EDITED BY BOB PATIENCE

ARROW BOOKS

Arrow Books Limited
62–65 Chandos Place, London WC2N 4NW

An imprint of Century Hutchinson Limited

London Melbourne Sydney Auckland
Johannesburg and agencies throughout
the world

First published by Stanley Paul & Co. Ltd 1986

Arrow edition 1987

Design by Shape of Things
Illustrations and front cover models
by Robin Bouttell

Typeset in Times Medium by
Avocet Marketing Services, Bicester, Oxon
Illustrations reproduced by
York House Graphics Ltd, London
Printed and bound in Great Britain by
Anchor Brendon Limited, Tiptree, Essex

ISBN 0 09 955060 1

CONTENTS

1 THE SAINT REMEMBERS SHANKLY

Liverpool had five superstars in the sixties. There were the Beatles and there was Bill Shankly. And probably had anyone asked John, Paul, George and Ringo to name their hero they might well have chorused 'Shanks'.

The man had magic. Bill Shankly's guidance of Liverpool FC, from the murky depths of second division football to numerous titles and world acclaim are well enough chronicled to justify the 'Great' tag accorded him by his peers. Shankly's dedication to, and love of football was something to behold. I was lucky enough to witness his qualities at close hand. Someone once asked Shankly about a certain match – was it 'a matter of life and death'? Said Shankly, 'It's far more serious than that, son'! Humour and dedication, with Shankly, went hand in hand.

I don't know who likened my old guv'nor to Jimmy Cagney – it might have been Shanks himself for I think he quite enjoyed the comparison – but whoever it was he got it spot on. For Shankly was like Cagney, a larger than life figure. A bristle-topped tough guy who used to keep my old Liverpool colleagues, myself and anyone else who cared to listen, enthralled, and at times, in stitches with his vast array of tales, explanations and descriptions of players, clubs and officials.

Certainly I will never forget my first introduction to the man who was to play such a major part in my footballing life. The year was 1960 and I was a part-time player with Motherwell earning only sixteen pounds a week – despite already having played for Scotland at full international level! Towards the end of the season '59–'60 I asked for a transfer from Fir Park, knowing full well that Newcastle United were interested in signing me. I had been tapped by the Geordies who were then managed by Charlie Mitten. On the evening Motherwell granted my request, I was already practising the Bladon Races as I stepped onto Fir Park to face Hamilton Accies in a Lanarkshire Cup tie.

If my memory is correct I scored a hat-trick in a match that Motherwell won easily – but I had Tyneside on my mind as I prepared to leave the ground. Then our manager, Bobby Ancell, said 'Sit where you are . . . there's a club here to talk to you.'

I was alone in the dressing room when Shankly came striding in. I couldn't help but be impressed by the man. He stood in front of me, a fit-looking character, hands deep in the pockets of a black crombie coat, the symbolic red tie under a sparkling white collar and, in true Cagney style, he hit me with a machine gun volley: 'Hello son . . . now how would you like to come to Liverpool? We're going to be the greatest team in the Country! You come to us. We've the greatest supporters. We've the greatest training ground. Come with me, tomorrow, to Liverpool. And bring your wife.'

At the time I couldn't even have told you what division Liverpool were in, but his spiel swept me right off my feet. The man was so dynamic I never even asked what every player wants to know – what would be in my wage packet!

I was mesmerised by the man and agreed to meet him back at the ground in the morning to travel to Liverpool with my wife Betsy. But that night, as Betsy and I were discussing the trip south, a knock came to the door; it was Charlie Mitten of Newcastle. He had been waiting in the street for me to come home. When I told him of Shankly he said: 'Don't go there lad. Come to Newcastle. We're first

division, they're only second. Tell that Shankly you're not going anywhere but Newcastle.'

Mitten's offer was a good one but it was hard to dismiss Shankly from the mind. In the morning though, after a sleepless night, I met Shanks in the back seat of a Liverpool director's Rolls Royce and shame-faced said I wanted to think things over. At that moment fate and Bobby Ancell took a hand. As I sat in the car, making excuses, Ancell came up to me and said: 'Either you go to Liverpool or you're staying here. One place you're not going is Newcastle. Liverpool have done everything right in their approach to Motherwell. If you don't sign for Bill you aren't signing for anyone.' It was an embarrassing moment for, naive as I was, I didn't think that Ancell knew anything of the Newcastle interest. Shankly, always positive, grabbed the opportunity: 'Stay in the car son. We'll pick up your wife and go to Liverpool.'

And that really was that. He had me hook, line and striker. At the time the journey to Liverpool, minus motorway, was five hours. But Shankly filled the time with stories about the club, players, fans and how we were going to be the best in the country. By the time I reached Anfield I think I knew all of my new team-mates intimately, even though I had never met them.

A quick look around a club house only had me grabbing for the pen to sign. I was Shankly's biggest buy at £37,500 and according to him I was lucky to be joining a team of superstars and getting a wage of £30 per week. He was right of course, but even then I never imagined the fun I was in for as well. And that was free.

Everyone has their favourite Shankly stories many of which have been embellished a little over the years. True or not, I've certainly had a few good dinners on the strength of them. Shanks brightened up our lives as players. Tommy Smith, Roger Hunt, Ron Yeats, Ian Callaghan, Peter Thompson, Geoff Strong, Tommy Lawrence, Chris Lawlor, Billy Stevenson and myself were Shankly's Boys and, because we helped him achieve success for Liverpool, he treated us like family. He was strict enough with us

but he always had an excuse whenever any of us went astray.

Typical was the occasion when Ron Yeats and myself got in a bit of hot water after a trip to the Republic of Ireland. We had played in a friendly match in Dublin and, as usual, the Irish pushed the boat out with the after-match hospitality. Shanks had put an eleven o'clock curfew on us all and Bob Paisley, then trainer, was the late watchdog to make sure everyone clocked in on time. By eleven o'clock most of the lads had checked in and by half past Shanks joined Bob in the Hotel foyer to check the roll call.

'All in but Yeats and St John,' said Bob. Shanks, realising that big Ronnie and I were enjoying the porter and sing-song somewhere growled at the news: 'Well you might as well get to bed Bob . . . those Scots will no be in for hours.' Shanks was right. Big Ronnie and I crept in a few hours later in good form but knowing full well there would be repercussions in the morning. Sure enough Shanks wouldn't look our way in the morning but Bob told us before departure: 'You two are in front of the gaffer when we get back.'

By the time we reached the plane the pleasing effects of the night before had turned into the hangover of the morning after. But we were still sharp enough to realise that we had to present a united front to the Boss when we returned to Anfield. Since Big Ron was the club skipper he had to face the music first, at least that's what I told him, but when he was eventually summonsed I had my ear to the door listening to the story, intent of course on absolute duplication.

Said Ron: 'Well it was like this Boss. You know these Irish, they kept plying us with drink after the game.' Shankly, a non-drinker, and by this time looking for an excuse to let us off growled: 'Ron, son, you should know the Irish by this time. Wild men with the drink. You shouldn't be led by them. But what kept you so late?' 'Well Boss' said Ron, warming to the tale, 'once we had a few drinks they invited us for a game of cards.' Shanks interrupted: 'What did I tell you. Wild men, drunks and gamblers. That's the Irish for you son. But you were still four hours late.' 'Yes Boss,' replied Yeatsie, 'but Saint and I were losing and we stayed on to try and win our money back.'

As I peeked around the door I could see Shanks shake his head and say: 'Son what have I told you – stay away from the Irish, card sharks, bad influence on everyone. Now let this be a lesson and don't let it happen again.'

I thought to myself 'Well done big man – we've cracked it' as I could hear Ron say: 'OK, Boss. Will I send Saint in now?'

To which Shanks replied: 'No need to son. No doubt he'll tell me the same ****ing pack of lies.'

Shanks was a one-off. His stories about players old and new were marvellous and as we grew to know him we milked the tales of Tom Finney (his favourite player), Stanley Matthews, Peter Doherty and the players he competed against when captain of Preston. Many a rainy morning we evaded training by cornering him in the tactics room at Anfield, merely mentioning a name and letting him rave about or demolish old-timers' abilities.

Of course the Boss was a fine player in his own right, a strong, forceful wing-half in a Preston team which included the great Finney. He was fiercely proud of his Scottish international caps and of his reputation as one of the toughest players of his time. One stormy day he was holding court when he remembered one of the young sensations of the thirties – Boy Baston of Arsenal, who, I suppose, was the equivalent of Trevor Steven of Everton today.

'You know Lads I was never one to take liberties you understand, but this fellow was a bit special. He came with a big reputation and being only a boy I didn't want any nonsense from him – me being an international player you see. So at the first throw-in I went to mark him and I whispered in his ear "none of your tricks son or you'll finish up on the track." But he didn't pay any attention and jinked inside me and away. At the next throw-in I got to him and hissed "any more of that boy and you'll be in real trouble" – but this time he turned me inside out and away he went again.

'In fact he beat me all ends up all through the first half despite me trying as hard as I could to intimidate him. I couldn't understand it at all until I mentioned to another Arsenal player at half-time how brave Batson was, ignoring my attempts to verbally intimidate him.

'But he laughed at me and said: "Don't you know Bill – the lad's stone deaf"!'

As our team progressed so did Shankly and so, of course, did the stories surrounding him. The training ground was his domain. He still longed for his playing days and every morning he would join us in the six-a-side match which always marked the end of the day's training. Shanks, like most Scots, hated losing. Often he would change sides half-way through a training match so he would finish on the winning team.

I well remember one occasion when it all went wrong for him. The game was tight, 5–5 I think, and there was a disputed decision against a Shanks side which included one of the quiet men of Anfield, Chrissie Lawlor. There was doubt about the ball having gone under the bar (two cricket stumps) and since it would have been the winning and final goal of the session Shanks was up in arms protesting to Bob Paisley, Ronnie Moran and Reuben Bennett about the goal being given. Everyone but the boss felt the ball had gone in but as a last throw he said: 'All right, we'll bring in a man whose integrity is never in doubt. A man of few words who'll tell the truth – Chrissie Lawlor. Now Chris, son, your honest opinion . . . was the ball over the line?'

'It was a goal boss,' replied Chris. We held back our laughter, awaiting the explosion. Sure enough Shanks blew: 'Can you believe that?' He shouted. 'I've waited ten years for the man to open his mouth and the first thing he tells me is a lie!' Exit an enraged Shankly leaving behind a pitch full of top-class footballers doubled up with laughter.

As I have mentioned Shankly's team talks in our little tactics room were something special. There was just about enough room for the twelve players plus Bob Paisley and Reuben Bennett when the boss held court before a big match. Usually his briefings ended up in laughter.

He used to be at the head of a table which was laid out, Subbuteo style, with opposition players and ourselves. On one occasion, when the great Manchester United side of the sixties was due to visit, Shankly was in splendid form. As usual he was impressing on us how good we were and how poor the opposition was. 'Now boys' he said, 'United tomorrow. I'll be surprised if they turn up at all we're playing so well. Matt might well keep them in Manchester and concede the points.' He then proceeded to eliminate the opposition with comments such as 'Alex Stepney – couldn't catch a cold. Tony Dunne – couldn't tackle a fish supper. Shay Brennan – you know somebody told me Matt has a bad back, I'll tell you he's got two bad backs! And Billy Foulkes? St John, you'll get a hat-trick – I've seen a juggernaut turn quicker than Foulkes. Nobby Stiles – I've a gnome in my garden bigger than him. And he's bloody blind as well. Paddy Crerand – now boys, Crerand's deceptive – he's slower than you think.'

All the time he had been removing the figures from the table and as we looked on he realised there were only three left – Law, Best and Charlton. Thinking quickly as the sniggers got louder he turned to us and said: 'There you are boys you've only three men to beat – and if you can't do that you don't deserve to be professional footballers!' United, a superb team, had the last laugh. They beat us 4–0!

Until recently Liverpool players have accepted European football as a fact of life. For years, up until the 1985/6 season, the fixture list has been lit up by continental opposition. But in the early sixties, when European soccer was a novelty to us all, Shankly was enthralled by the thought of playing foreign opposition. I remember one famous tactics room occasion. We had been drawn against Honved in the European Cup and the boss, as usual wanting to make sure everything was right, sent Reuben Bennett over to spy on the Hungarians. In those days that was a four-day trip and when Reuben reappeared after travelling all over Europe by plane, boat and train, he was armed with a dossier on Honved that would have filled an encyclopaedia.

Shanks gathered us together and enthused about Honved. 'Boys, this is it. The European Cup. This is what it's all about. Honved from Hungary. The team with a name. Puskas played for them. The great teams they've had.' At this point Reuben weighed down with his dossier piped up: 'And I'll tell you something lads, they've got a good team now too.' Shanks quickly jumped in, 'Reuben... we're not interested in them. It's how we play – forget all that.' Poor Reuben had spent four days trekking round Europe for nothing!

Reuben, by the way, was a marvellous character too. A former Dundee goalkeeper, he had been my trainer at Motherwell in the early years and was one of the first faces I ever met at Anfield. It was nice to meet an old friend at Anfield and I grew to enjoy his stories too.

One hilarious tale from his early days came when he played for a junior side in the Scottish Highlands. In those days there was no telephone to relay a score back to a village or a newspaper when a little team won, but each side took a carrier pigeon to fly news of a score home. On the day in question Reuben's team won a notable victory in the Scottish Junior Cup, and such was the excitement amongst the team that it was decided that Big Wullie, the club's most loyal fan, who travelled everywhere with the team, should have the honour of releasing the bird to wing the great news home to their village. Big Wullie excited by the result and the honour was duly given the pigeon which he lifted to his lips and shouted 'We won, two–one.' He then released it into the heavens as the club secretary stood dumbfounded with the piece of paper which should have been pinned to its leg!

Another Scottish story comes from a trip to Iceland, and the day Shanks took us all to Butlins!

It was in the early days of European football and air travel was not as sophisticated as it is today. We were due to play in Reykjavik and the plane we boarded at Speke was so old we touched down at Carlisle to take on wood. Then Prestwick before we joined up with another plane for Iceland. Since there was a few hours delay, Shanks, Ayrshire born,

decided he would treat us all to a trip to the Butlins Holiday camp at Ayr. 'A marvellous place boys. My wife Nessie and I often had our holidays there,' he told us as we headed off by coach. As we approached the holiday camp an attendant came to the camp barrier and halted us. Quick as a flash Shanks was out of the coach. 'Liverpool Football Club, travelling to Reykjavik,' he informed the attendant. 'Then I'm afraid you've taken the wrong turning sir,' said the man 'this is Butlins!' The boss's face was as red as his tie.

Bill Shankly was the man who moulded Liverpool into the force they are today in world football. He is also the man who began the updating of what is now one of the best stadiums in Europe. The boss was immensely proud of the ground. He liked nothing better than to give visiting pressmen a guided tour of the facilities. He would say: 'We've not only the best team, but the best stand. And look at the dressing rooms. You could have five-a-sides in here, no bother son. And what about the baths? I've seen smaller swimming pools than that.'

On one occasion his obsession with having the best went over the top. He ushered the press party into the toilets flushed one and then stated proudly: 'There you are lads, filled in fifteen seconds – a world record!'

The treatment room was a constant source of unlikely stories – one of which involved me!

On a Saturday before a vital mid-week cup match I had disgraced myself by being sent off at Coventry following a dust-up with Brian Lewis. Shanks was beside himself. At that time an errant player had to appear before a Football Association disciplinary committee and there was no doubt that on the Monday I was for the high-jump: the ordering off was not my first offence. It meant that I would be missing from the cup tie and so Shanks set out to tilt the scales of justice in Liverpool's favour.

Every Sunday the boss held court at Anfield to the local and national press, giving them his views on everything from the referee to the price of tea. But it was unusual for players to be called in so I was surprised when I was sent for. I was even more surprised when I was ordered onto the treatment table, told to drop my trousers, and Bob Paisley was instructed to start applying a mixture of gentian violet and black boot polish around my private parts. What worried me further was that Bob was beginning to enjoy his artwork until the boss said 'Enough . . . that'll do fine.' Then to my astonishment he hurled the treatment room door open and ushered in the waiting press saying, 'There, take a look at that lads . . . if that was not intimidation enough to make any man hit back I don't know what is.' The sly old fox kept the suddenly interested scribes just far enough away to be suitably impressed by the apparent damage, and the next morning the papers were full of the brutal attack on Ian St John which had prompted the Saturday punch-up. As we travelled to London for the tribunal Shanks chuckled at the coverage: 'There's no way they can suspend you after this lot son! You'll be playing on Wednesday night.'

He was laughing on the other side of his face as the committee – rightly – found me guilty as charged and suspended me for fourteen days. I had lost my case, and my dignity as well!

Shankly, of course, was a great manager and like all the greats he could spot a player a mile away. It should be remembered that he would scour the lower divisions in England and Scotland and come up with gems . . . Kevin Keegan and Ray Clemence, both from Scunthorpe, are two major stars in recent years who spring immediately to mind. Another player who blossomed under Shanks was Alex Lindsay, who was bought from Bury at the behest of Bob Paisley. Alex eventually became an international full-back, but in the early days in training the boss had him playing in mid-field and he was having a nightmare time. After watching Alex for a fortnight Shanks decided it was time for a pep talk. He took Alex aside, put his arm around his shoulders, and said: 'Now Alex, I want you to do what you did at Bury . . . take men on in the penalty area and shoot at goal whenever you get the chance.' Replied Alex: 'That wasn't me boss, that was Jimmy Kerr.' 'Nonsense' snorted Shanks, 'you were the man who used to make those great runs from mid-field, played marvellous one-twos and were as sharp as a tack before goal.' Again Alex replied: 'No boss, that was Jimmy Kerr.' – to which Shanks turned to Bob Paisley, still with his arm around Alex's shoulders, and said 'My god Bob, we've signed the wrong player.'

During my time at Liverpool under Shankly we progressed from being second division players to League title holders and ambassadors for football around the world. On one tour to the United States, Shanks' enthusiasm and suspicion of foul play rebounded on him.

It was in the days when there was no professional football on the other side of the Atlantic and, as League champions, we were showing the flag to the Yanks and the Canadians. Also on tour at the same time was the West German side, Mydrecke. Following two really tough games in Chicago and San Francisco against them – one won and one drawn – we met for the third time in Vancouver. It was a real battle and I was sent off following trouble with a large, blond centre-half. Coming off, Ron Yeats, who was in plaster following an earlier injury, was laughing as I reached the bench. 'What's the joke?' I asked. 'Well I'm laughing at you getting in trouble again,' said Ronnie. I countered by saying: 'Anyway I'm glad I'm off – that ball is like a cannonball – my head is sore from heading it.' At that Big Ron burst into more laughter: 'No wonder,' he said. 'The boss was convinced that the German keeper had been letting air out of the ball every time he touched it. When it comes over here he and Reuben have been pumping air into it. It's now so hard it's like a rock.'

The match finished with Shanks screaming at the Germans, and reminding them that they hadn't beaten us in three games and that was on top of us winning two wars. Diplomacy was never one of his strong points. But again the joke was on him. The next day we moved on to Toronto for another match while he flew home to Britain early. And just guess who he travelled back with... yes, that's right, the Germans!

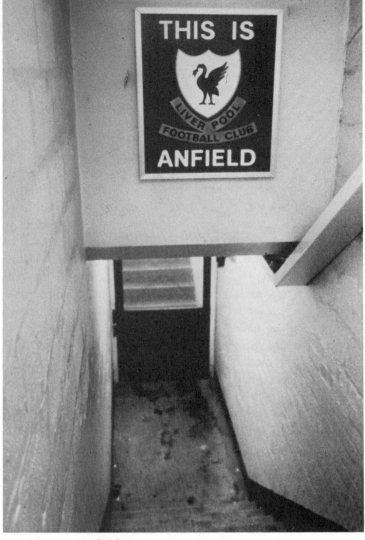

● *The famous Anfield sign*

If Bill Shankly had not been a footballer he would have been a boxer; boxing was his second love and he never let us forget it. During my ten years at Liverpool our pre-match, after-match and day-before-match meal was always steak, 'Because,' Shanks would say 'Joe Louis trained on steak – so it must be good for you.'

As I've said the Boss did like to get his own way and his love of boxing meant disappointment one night for two old ladies who just happened to be staying in one of our stopover hotels. It was in the days when Muhammad Ali was really making a name for himself and on the night in question his fight was live on TV, at 7.30 in the evening. All the way to our hotel all Shanks could do was talk about the fight and we, too, were excited at the thought of seeing Ali at his best. In those days there were no individual television sets in rooms, only a TV lounge. So, after the compulsory steak and chips we all strolled into the TV lounge only to find the two old dears settling down to watch Coronation Street, which was in direct opposition.

Shanks duly breezed in, asking why the fight wasn't on; we pointed out the two pensioners sitting in front of the set. It was time for desperate measures and Shanks took them. He approached the old women and said: 'Now we've got to be democratic here. Hands up all those who want to see the fight.' Naturally the entire team, and himself, voted for Ali. 'Now who wants to see Coronation Street?' Up went the hands of the two old ducks. 'Motion carried,' said Shanks, as two Coronation Street fans left the room looking just a little bit disgruntled over the technical knock-out.

My final Shankly story is of the day he silenced Supermac – Malcolm Macdonald, then of Newcastle United. The famous sign *This Is Anfield* in the players' tunnel was put there by Shankly – a last-second reminder to opposition of exactly where they are doing battle. I am sure that the sign has frightened many a player over the years. To my mind it is a masterly piece of Shankly psychology.

But one day, when Newcastle United were visiting, Supermac annoyed Shankly intensely with his remarks about the legendary notice. Shanks was always at his best on match days. He sparkled at the thought of a game and he was always on hand to greet the opposition. He would start with a bit of banter with the opposition's manager – on this occasion Joe Harvey – and drop in a word of warning for opposing players. It was an act, his schoolboyish enthusiasm for football bubbling over.

But as Macdonald entered with Harvey he spotted the *This Is Anfield* notice and quipped 'I see we've found the right ground then boss.' It was a typical cocky Macdonald remark but Shankly saw it as a lack of respect and stormed into our dressing room saying: 'Lads, that Macdonald has been taking the mickey out of the club. He's been mocking Anfield, and he should be taught a lesson.' His psychology, if that's what it was, worked. The team went out and thrashed United five–nil, and at the end of the game Shankly dashed straight down from his seat in the Stand to the Newcastle dressing room. As Joe Harvey looked up from trying to console shattered players Shanks growled 'Where's Macdonald?' Supermac, like the rest of the Newcastle boys, was stunned but Shanks rounded on him saying: 'Well I don't think you'll forget where Anfield is now son, will you?'

That was Shankly. Unable to curb his pride, enthusiasm and passion for the game he had loved since a lad in a mining family in Glenbuck, Ayrshire.

Shanks was a master of his craft and every player who was touched by him will never forget him. It was one of the saddest days of my life when he was taken from us prematurely in the Autumn of 1979. The game had lost a great, and we who had lived and laughed with him had lost a friend. The memories and stories, though, will never leave us.

2 GREAVSIE AND GUVNORS

never had the pleasure of playing under the late, great Bill Shankly but I remember well his humour... and his knack of building up his own team and demolishing the opposition with one withering statement. As any Liverpool – or Tottenham – fan will tell you, until 1985 Spurs had not won at Anfield since 1912, and that was the year the Titanic went down! I can tell you that plenty of good Spurs sides went under at Liverpool almost as spectacularly as that infamous liner, and Shanks was always quick to remind anyone who was around of that fact.

Our Spurs side was pretty useful. You don't have players such as Cliff Jones, Dave Mackay, Danny Blanchflower, Maurice Norman, John White and, although I say it myself, Jimmy Greaves in a line-up without fancying yourselves a bit. But Shanks had his own name for us, and I'll never forget it – 'The Drury Lane Fan Dancers'. To him it summed up the soft London life we were supposed to live. We didn't used to take it seriously, but every time we visited Anfield it was dear old Bill who'd have the last laugh.

Mind you, even though I didn't serve under Shanks I did have my fair share of memorable guvnors, including, of course, two knights of the realm Sir Walter Winterbottom, and the much-misunderstood Sir Alf Ramsey.

My first guvnor was Ted Drake at Chelsea. I joined Chelsea at 16 and, of course, was very much in awe of the great Drake – the man who once scored seven goals for the Arsenal in one game. Ted was of the old brigade of managers, strictly a collar and tie man, and one you seldom saw near the training pitch. The great man kept himself to himself but on occasion he wasn't averse to giving a fair bit of stick.

I remember one occasion I got it hot and hefty... and I wasn't even playing! It was in my second year as a first-team player and we drew fourth division Darlington in the Cup. The first match was at Stamford Bridge and we had a nightmare, only drawing with the North-East side. It was a bit of a disaster, and I was dropped for the return match. The replay wasn't much better but at the end of 90 minutes the score was 1–1 and, of course, everyone expected the fitter, more experienced first division Chelsea to go on and clinch things in extra time. But football, as I keep saying, is a funny old game. We finished up losing 4–1 in one of the sensations of the season.

In those days there were no substitutes – only a travelling reserve in case of emergencies. That was me and when I went into the dressing room the Boss was giving the lads a real roasting. I felt relatively safe; after all I hadn't been part of the debacle but spotting me he turned and gave me my first-ever dressing down in football roaring at me: 'And as for you Greaves, it shows you what kind of ****ing player you are, you can't even get in this side!' I was eighteen and on the way to realising that football can do funny things even to gentlemen.

I always had respect for Ted Drake although he didn't communicate much with us. He left all the spade work to Albert Tennent our trainer and Jack Oxbury our coach. I never once saw Ted Drake in a track suit although I did, on occasion, catch him in a golf shirt. He was rather adept at nipping off for his game of golf!

Chelsea in those days was a fun club to be with. We were free spirits in fact we were known as the "All The Best" club simply because that was all people would say to us as we went onto the field...

no tactics talks just 'all the best'. We were always fighting relegation yet we used to score near enough a hundred goals a season. The problem was we let in nearly a hundred as well! I liked Chelsea and would never have left them had the maximum wage ban been lifted before I was contracted to AC Milan. Milan had signed an option on me halfway through season 1959/60, their manager at the time, Guiseppe Vianni, being very keen for me to try my hand at Italian football. He then had a heart attack and had to retire with the result that the new man, Nereo Rocco, brought in from Padova, inherited me. I don't think he appreciated that. Rocco was a wartime partisan – don't ask me on what side – and was a real hard man.

By the time it came for me to finally sign I wanted out. The maximum wage had been abolished. My old mate Johnny Haynes was earning £100 a week and I fancied a bit of that without leaving dear Old Blighty. Chelsea promised to try and get me out of the deal, even to the extent of sending one of their lawyers to Alassio with me to talk to the then Milan president Signor Spaduccini.

Actually looking back I'm convinced that Chelsea never wanted the deal to be scrapped. I remember well walking down Alassio High Street with the solicitor Chelsea had sent. He was as out of place as jellied eels at a Windsor Castle banquet with his bowler hat, stiff collar, striped trousers, rolled umbrella and tails – little wonder the Italians in the street cafes were choking on their chianti.

At the end of a couple of days wrangling my lawyer friend informed me that I couldn't get out of the contract but that he had got me a better deal. Chelsea were £80,000 the richer and I was on a collision course with my new boss, Signor Rocco, the man Desmond Hackett of the *Daily Express* once described as 'an overweight, ex-heavyweight boxer'. Over the nine months I didn't actually come to blows with Rocco – I wasn't that daft – but I made myself the bane of his life. Rocco treated his players like, I suppose, he treated his patriots during the war. He was tough, no respector of persons and, to be brutal, a horrible man. I don't think Rocco knew

(MIL-4)Milan,Italy,Sept.24(AP)-British soccer sta
Jimmy Greaves in action against Bernasconi (left)
and Bergamaschi(right) of the 'Sampdoria' soccer
team here today. The 'Milan' club in which Greaves
plays, lost 2-3. Jimmy scored twice(AP WIREPHOTO)
mm/rs Sept.24 Str. Olympia

what to do with me. I arrived disgruntled at having been lumbered with a team and a country I didn't want anything to do with. I was also a few days late for the pre-season training because I had waited in England until my daughter Mitzi was born. Rocco immediately fined me, I think around £100, which in those days was a hell of a lot of money.

And things didn't improve. I refused to bow and scrape to him and I was fined every time I shuffled out of line which I must admit was often. I once went to Venice with my wife Irene and was fined £400 – ridiculous when you think of it – and that, would you believe it, was exactly the bonus Rocco put on the team winning the Milan derby that week against Inter. We won the game but I lost the bonus. After that Rocco used to fine me for skipping the fence in training camps, having a cigarette, having a drink on the Q.T. and I found I was playing for virtually nothing.

What people didn't realise was that while the signing on fee in those days in Italian soccer was good – around £20,000 – it spread over, say, three years of your contract. In fact the wages weren't much better than back home, around £30 per week. By the time my bonuses were taken off, and the fines taken off, I was finishing up skint – not exactly the situation I had envisaged when I signed.

It was Rocco who was the problem. I thought I was a success in Italy, scoring eleven goals in 13 games. But before Bill Nicholson stepped in to bring me back to Spurs for that ridiculous £99,999 fee I was made to feel like an intruder. The Milan team was pretty good in those days and the fans were always on my side. I enjoyed their company and they enjoyed my play. This is more than can be said for some of my team-mates, especially those who were terrified of Rocco. The team actually went on to win the European Cup the year after I left with players like Gianni Rivera, Trappatoni, Altafini and Maldini.

Until I decided I had had enough, I got on OK with them. But in my last game Rocco was in a spot.

● *Who's a pretty boy! Here I am holding my AC Milan shirt*

He couldn't leave me out because of my goal-scoring, but I'm convinced he told the other players not to give me the ball so that I would leave under a cloud. But I spoiled his plans. It was against one of the lower clubs in the league and, in a goalmouth scramble, I poked in a goal. I turned round to get my congratulations and every player had his head down – not one had the bottle to say 'well done'.

Mind you, while the memory lingers, at the time I couldn't care less. I was on my way back to England to join Tottenham Hotspur, the double winning side and yet another guvnor... Bill Nicholson.

People seem to have the entirely wrong idea about Bill Nicholson. His image is of a somewhat dour Yorkshireman but in fact I always found Bill the complete gentleman. He didn't say much but he let his teams do the talking, and in the early sixties our team virtually picked itself.

And Bill was big enough to admit when he'd made a mistake. I remember our pre-match tactics talk before we played Athletico Madrid in the 1961 European Cup Winners Cup Final in Rotterdam. Naturally we were all a bit nervous and Bill – unlike Shankly started to praise the opposition players to the heights.

We were beginning to believe that the goalkeeper had six pairs of hands, that Milton and Djalmar Santos, the great Brazilian full-backs had only learned their skills from the Athletico back pair, their half-back line was fantastic and their forwards didn't bear thinking about. I remember us beginning to feel we were facing supermen and the atmosphere in the dressing room was getting decidedly edgy when Danny Blanchflower, who was only in the side because Dave Mackay was injured, actually saved the day by piping up in his Irish brogue: 'Hold on a minute boss. Can you imagine their team talk?' Bill asked: 'What do you mean Danny?' And Danny, God bless him, said: 'Their manager will be saying – "lads we're up against it here – Maurice Norman, England centre-half, Cliff Jones, the fastest winger in the world, John White one of the games' greatest inside forwards, Jimmy Greaves up front, Bobby Smith, a tank of a striker..." and so on. Can you imagine boss – they must be frightened out of their minds facing us.' Suddenly the atmosphere in the dressing room was transformed. I looked round the room and everyone was saying: 'Danny's dead right, let's have a go at these people.' And the boss too realised that Danny was right. We went out that night and totally destroyed Athletico Madrid. Winning 5–1, we became the first British team to win a European trophy. It was Danny's pep talk that changed our attitude and Bill Nick was big enough to realise this.

Bill Nicholson had a sense of humour alright, but really it was the Spurs players I had most fun with and I well remember one occasion shortly after the double winning side had been split up. Bill Nick had brought in Eddie Bailey as coach. Eddie was a hard case who did love a road race, particularly when he was up front directing traffic on a bicycle!

Now certain players can road race – some can't . . . and some won't. Alan Gilzean and myself were in the third category and I remember one misty morning on the roads around Cheshunt when Bailey, who fancied himself a bit of a sergeant major was giving the tail enders, who I remember consisted of myself, Gillie and Pat Jennings, then a mere stripling, a taste of some barrack-room language exhorting us, shall we say, to greater efforts. As we reached the banks of the River Lea we had had enough. We pulled Eddie off his bike and then threw it into the River, leaving Eddie shouting for help as we galloped off towards Cheshunt and the showers.

Poor Eddie. My last memory was of him trying to get help as he attempted to fish his bicycle out of the river. Strange to say there were no repercussions. Eddie was never quite as rude to us again and Bill Nicholson never said a word. I've a feeling the guvnor probably had a quiet chuckle himself.

It was during my time with Spurs that I gathered most of my international caps. I have some funny memories of the men who guided me in the white shirt of England. One man for whom I have special affection is Joe Mercer, who at one time ran the England Under-23 side. Joe always seemed to have a smile on his face and was always good for a laugh.

He told me a few stories of the old days and one I loved concerned the one time referee Dennis Howell who went on to become the Labour Minister for Sport. It was in the days when old Joe was Aston Villa's manager and one of his key defenders was a famous scouser Jimmy Dugdale. Villa were playing Preston at a time when Tom Finney – Bill Shankly's favourite player – was in his prime. Finney, playing at centre-forward, gave Dugdale a real roasting and after he had shown him a clean pair of heels for around the twentieth time in the match he shouted in desperation 'Off-side ref, off-side.' Howell would have none of it and waved play on. 'You must be bloody blind ref' claimed Dugdale. Howell wheeled round and said: 'What was that Dugdale?' To which the irrepresible Dugdale countered: 'Lord help us don't tell me you're deaf as well!'

Joe Mercer could give advice too, and he brought me down to earth once as a youngster when I joined him for an Under-23 training session before a Scotland match. Joe, an old fox, noticed I was a bit out of sorts, put his arm around me and asked: 'What's up Greavsie, you look a bit down?' I told Joe that I was a bit worried. I had lost my scoring touch and was beginning to wonder if it would ever come back. He tried to console me saying 'That happens to every striker son, now tell me how many have you scored already this season?' 'Thirty-six' I replied to which Joe replied, 'Thirty-six, and you're looking for sympathy . . . go about your business Greaves.' You know it worked. He made me realise that I was luckier than most and from what I remember I went on to score in the under-23 match.

One other great story about Joe which I am told is absolutely true concerns a fairly well-known pressman who phoned him when Manchester City were going through a particularly sticky spell. Commiserating with Joe but still looking for a story his last question was: 'Have you thought of signing anyone Joe?' The reply was a little muffled but the writer had his story. On the back page in bold headlines was the story *City To Go For Ernie Hunt*. The writer involved was sitting reading his work over breakfast well pleased at the scoop when the

phone rang. It was a very irate Joe Mercer on the other end of the line. 'What the bloody hell are you trying to do, writing that I am ready to pay that kind of money for Ernie Hunt. I've never even thought about the lad. My directors and Coventry City will go mad about this.' The writer, mystified, countered: 'But Joe, I asked you yesterday who you fancied signing and you said Ernie Hunt.' There was a pause at the other end of the line and then roaring through came Joe: 'I didn't say "Ernie Hunt" you idiot, I said "Any C . . ."'! Knowing Joe he would have soon seen the humour in the incident. He was one of my favourite characters in the game.

It was Walter Winterbottom who introduced me to international football and you know when people talk to me about the Munich disaster, when all those marvellous Manchester United players died in the aircrash, I always think how Winterbottom suffered along with Sir Matt Busby. It's worth remembering that on that disastrous day back in 1958 not only United but English greats perished. The marvellous Duncan Edwards, Tommy Taylor, Roger Byrne, Eddie Colman, David Pegg – all great players with long international careers before them.

Walter was the civil servant who was a bit ahead of his time in football coaching terms. He did get a knighthood but he never did get the job he wanted – Secretary of the Football Association. That was a pity for he was probably the right man for the job. He certainly built a fine England side and, as I say, had the Munich air disaster never happened then perhaps he and not a later guvnor of mine, Alf Ramsey, would have guided an England team to World Cup glory.

Walter was a great thinker about the game and he used to go through his personally developed routines with players. My usual reaction after a five minute tactics talk was: 'Would you mind repeating that Walter?' Walter used to give me a quizzical look as if

● *England v. Wales, 1948. Back row (left to right): Leuty (reserve), Scott, Aston, W. Winterbottom (manager), Swift, Wright (captain), Ward, H. Bourne (trainer). Front row (left to right): Matthews, Mortensen, Milburn, Shackleton, Finney, Franklin.*

he wasn't quite sure whether I was taking the rise or not. I wasn't – he used to leave me bewildered with some of his ideas. It was comforting to know that the great Len Shackleton had the same problem some time before me – although he once did give Walter some cheek!

It was the great England team of the fifties... Shackleton, Mortensen, Ramsey, Wright, Finney... they were all there one day as Walter's brain moved into overdrive. He started off talking to England keeper Gil Merrick saying: 'Gil, when you get the ball throw it to Alf (Ramsey). Alf you push it down the line to Stan (Matthews). Stan – a little jink with Ernie Taylor, a one-two, take the full-back on, and square it back for Len (Shackleton). Len I want you coming in on the edge of the box knocking it in the back of the net.' And Len, the clown prince of soccer, lived up to his title asking: 'Any particular side Walter?'

That was Walter and the early days of coaching. It was all in Walter's head. Then, as now, you still have to execute the best thought plans on the pitch. And believe me that isn't easy.

Walter Winterbottom was, and still is, a fine man. He was a thinker and, in many ways, the founder of modern football as we know it. It's hard to believe now but that was only 25 years ago yet Walter, though England manager, didn't have the right to pick the team. The selection committee did that. What a way to run a circus! Would the other 'Sir', Alf Ramsey, have flourished under this system... more of that later!

At club level my last senior guvnor was another man who went on to run his country. This was Ron Greenwood, then of West Ham. Ron was a nice man who throughout his management career, had built fine footballing sides. Unfortunately, the accusation was always held against them that they were a little on the soft side. Like my earlier move to AC Milan from Chelsea I was unhappy at moving to West Ham from Spurs. I was happy at White Hart Lane and would have readily played out my senior days there. It was a shock of the first order when one day I got a 'phone call to say: 'Get your boots – you're

going to West Ham.' The season was 1969/70 and mentally I was tired although, I did feel I had more goals in me for Spurs.

I was, and still am, bitter at the way I was informed that I was to be part of the deal which took Martin Peters to White Hart Lane and me to Upton Park. I realise that footballers are expendable at all times but I would have thought that anyone giving the kind of service I gave to Tottenham might have been given the hard news in a softer manner. The Hammers were having a bad time; relegation threatened. The fine team of the sixties was beginning to go over the hill and Martin Peters wisely saw the signs. Ron Greenwood got me plus £100,000 and it was back to the old Chelsea days of

26

● *F.A. Cup Final, 1962: Spurs v. Burnley. Victorious, we run round the pitch with the Cup*

trying to avoid the drop.

And avoid it we did. Ron put me straight in the side and we went to Maine Road to play Joe Mercer's Manchester City. We smashed them 5–1, and I got a couple. That sparked a little revival which eventually got us clear of trouble. Ron suddenly had that nice grin he always had as a player at Chelsea when I was a lad there. Mind you he wasn't smiling a year later when Bobby Moore and I got involved in the ill-fated Blackpool incident – something which cost the Hammers a Cup tie and which pointed me towards the 'Exit Door' of top class soccer.

If ever there was a storm in a lager glass it occurred in the first week of January 1971. West Ham United with the likes of Bobby Moore, Geoff Hurst, Clyde Best and Jimmy Greaves in their midst, and under the astute management of Ron Greenwood, had drawn Blackpool in the Third Round of the F.A. Cup at Bloomfield Road. On paper it looked a doddle for the Hammers. Instead the match not only gave Ron Greenwood a Ne'erday hangover any Scot would have been proud of, but also created a new guessing game in English football – guess the Fourth Man!

For those of you not old enough to remember one of the so-called soccer scandals of the seventies let me explain. Blackpool, as anyone knows, is famous for its tower, illuminations, landladies and rock. Not since the halcyon days of Matthews and Mortenson had it been renowned for it's football – that is not until January 3rd 1971. For that was the day which I suggest might be imprinted as indelibly in the mind of Ron Greenwood as the legend BLACKPOOL is stamped through the aforementioned candy delicacy.

Ron might have been encouraged that the draw against a clever, but not outstanding, Blackpool side which included that crafty little Scot Tony Green, might just prove a passport to the next round. Instead the trip to the north's favourite holiday resort turned into a public nightmare which certainly ruined my taste for football at its highest level and which brought unnecessary hurt to my old mate Bobby Moore. The story of the game itself will go down in the annals of Blackpool FC as one of their most famous victories of post-war years. I've always said that the game should not have been played, such was the state of the pitch, but nevertheless it was and we got slaughtered 4–0. Two things stick in my memory: I got the 'Top Star' award for West Ham in the *Sunday People* the next day, and Bobby Moore had the worst game I've ever seen him play!

Tony Green was magnificent that day. He ran Moore ragged and, at the end of a miserable ninety minutes, Blackpool had the result of the day. Naturally we were disappointed but good luck to them – that was the end of it we thought as we headed for the smoke.

But we soon had another thought coming. On the Wednesday following the match my wife Irene spotted a London newspaper board HAMMERS FOUR IN BLACKPOOL CLUB SENSATION. Being a knowledgeable soul she thought 'I wonder who the other one is?' She had clocked immediately that her husband, along with friends Bobby Moore and Brian Dear were bound to make up three of the sinners... but who could that fourth rascal be? She was not alone in her wonderment. Apparently, when the news broke, every other senior footballer in London had the same thought. I'm told that certain clubs even had a sweep going on who the fourth man would be! As it happened Public Enemy Number

Four was Clyde Best, that strong-running West Indian inside-forward who, in fact, was a totally innocent party in the whole inflated affair.

The story behind the headlines began on the Friday night, the eve of the Cup tie. We arrived at our hotel in Blackpool and before dinner Bobby Moore and I had a couple of lagers – nothing heavy you understand – only a couple of bottles. It was a situation I had become used to at West Ham. Tottenham had kept us under lock and key until match time but the Hammers were an easier-going lot... and who is to say they weren't right as West Ham played some great football during the Greenwood regime. It was after dinner, around ten o'clock, when Bobby Moore mentioned Brian London's club. The former British heavyweight's nightclub was a favourite sojourn for footballers... admittedly usually *after* a game. On that Friday night Bobby Moore, Brian Dear, Ron Jenkins (our physio), Clyde Best and I waited in the foyer for a few more clubmates – intent on sinking a couple of pints before bed. Luckily for the others they never joined us, for they too would have suffered at the hands of the press and the West Ham faithful a few days later. There isn't really much to tell about the visit to London's club. It was the day after New Year. The place was empty, there were no dolly birds around, we all had a few drinks and left. When I say 'drinks' I should mention that Clyde Best had been drinking pineapple juice all night. The big fellow was a dedicated young professional and he was blameless in the whole affair – yet he still took a backlash from which he never really fully recovered.

The storm broke on the Wednesday morning. Ron Greenwood, no doubt aware that the press had the scent of scandal in their nostrils, approached me at training and asked: 'Were you one of the lot who went clubbing on the night before the Blackpool match?' There was little point in lying. I answered: 'Yes'. That day, and for the following weeks, it seemed that the papers were full of it – how we had let the club down, how we had been drinking into the early hours of the morning before a vital match and all, of course, accompanied by pictures of Brian

London's club with the inevitable dolly birds.

Greenwood, whose season was in tatters anyway – we were close to the foot of the division and out of the Cup – fined us all two weeks wages and suspended us for a fortnight. I remember being disappointed in Ron. Not for myself but for Bobby Moore. I had only been at Upton Park a few months and deserved all I got for stepping out of line. But Bobby Moore had, for years, carried West Ham on his shoulders. He didn't deserve that kind of schoolboy reprimand. As for Clyde Best . . . he was absolutely innocent but was punished along with Brian Dear and myself. The fans, I felt, never gave him much support after that and that was a shame. He was a fine, big, honest player.

People still ask me whether I feel it was the booze that caused our poor form against Blackpool. The answer is, I honestly don't know. All I can say is that I don't put Bobby Moore's dreadful form down to having a few pints the night before. Mooro had gone through more lager than Carlsberg and was still one of the World's greatest. Since only three of us played, Bobby, myself and big Clyde, what the hell happened to the other eight who faced Tony Green and company. Had they gone to a better night club than us?

The escapade was only publicised because we were beaten, and because we were foolish enough to sit down with the other hotel guests for coffee and sandwiches on the eve of the game after our trip to London's. Had we won there would have been no stories, no scandal, no suspensions.

As it was the Hammers lost their next few matches and Greenwood was forced to bring Bobby and I back into the side two weeks later against Coventry. Bobby played a blinder and I scored the winner. Goals had been my trade but that one gave me special satisfaction. And as the ball hit the back of the net I did something I had never done before, I wheeled and gave the bench a 'V'-sign. Mr. Greenwood was not amused. We went on to escape relegation again but Blackpool was the beginning of the end for me. I retired at the end of the season. The glory days were over.

3 TEAM-MATES
— BY THE SAINT

eing an integral part of the great Liverpool team of the sixties, my club team-mates were nearly all full international players. They were also first class in providing memorable moments of fun and laughter.

Tommy Lawrence, the regular keeper during the glory years of Shanks' team was a real character. He has the dubious distinction of being one of the few men ever to con Bill Shankly – every week. Shanks, as everyone knows, was a teetotal non-smoker. He couldn't stop the lads having a drink but he was immensely proud of the fact that none of his players smoked – and he came out in press with that fact. What he didn't know was that Tommy, a fellow Scot, liked a fag and Tommy's ways of avoiding the boss to have a drag became a regular Saturday laugh-in with the rest of us. Our normal away schedule was lunch, tactics talk and then onto the team bus.

Shanks, of course, held court at both lunch and the tactics talk, but in the few minutes before boarding our coach, Tommy would nip off to have a sly puff. He got so devious that no-one could ever find him and we used to run a 'Spot the Goalie' sweep trying to catch him out. The strange thing is, no-one ever did. Thank goodness Shanks never did!

Tommy – a superb keeper – had a strange nickname. He was known as 'the Dipper', so called because of his ability to get into his bath, dress and be out the club door before the rest of us could get our boots off.

Our left back at Anfield was Gerry Byrne, a quiet man but one of the hardest men ever to pull on a boot and it was Gerry who caused a policy decision to be made at Anfield which has never been rescinded.

We were playing at Tottenham against Greavsie's lot and Gerry had taken up his position at the near post as the Spurs winger took an inswinging corner. For no apparent reason Gerry ducked and the ball flew straight into the net, costing us, if I remember correctly, the match. After the game Shankly almost burst the door open. 'Alright Byrne, what's your excuse?' he rasped. 'I heard someone say "duck" boss and I ducked,' answered the disconsolate Gerry. 'You ducked' blasted Shanks. 'Son, people have been put in Walton Jail for less than what you did out there today.' Gerry curled up in a corner and from that day on Shanks instilled in every team that you never ducked a ball at Liverpool. You headed, kicked or chested the ball away, no matter who shouted. It's a policy which I believe still holds firm today – and in retrospect it isn't a bad one.

Our other full back, Chrissie Lawlor, was so quiet he made Gerry Byrne seem positively garrulous. But Chris was a fabulous servant and I remember the occasion when he was due to play his 250th consecutive game for the club – an incredible record. During the week before the match Chrissie took an ankle knock and, as we moved on to shooting practice, Bob Paisley turned to him and said: 'Chrissie – we don't want you doing anything silly before Saturday; you go off and have a little jog. Don't take any chances.' Chris duly loped off but Shanks who was just arriving saw him jogging away from the group and demanded of Paisley: 'Bob, what's the matter with that malingerer Lawlor?' Poor Chris, 250 consecutive matches and branded a malingerer!

If Gerry Byrne was a tank of a player then Tommy Smith was a whole panzer division. Smiddy also had one of the quickest wits around, and referees, never his favourite people, were often at the wrong end of it. I remember two occasions when whistlers were left red-faced after typical Smithy attacks.

The first came at a time when the Football League, in their wisdom, had decided that referees should come into dressing rooms before matches and give teams a 'do's and dont's' talk. Tommy couldn't stand that and on one occasion took himself off to the toilet as a blushing referee tried to give us his spiel. 'What's that ref? Speak up!' shouted Tommy from the cubicle. As the ref raised his voice Tommy called again: 'Can't hear you in here, you'll need to speak louder than that.' The banter went on for five minutes after which the referee left blushing to the core. Odd thing was, we never saw that referee again.

Another official tried the soft sell. 'Listen lads, play the game out there... don't give me a hard time. After all I'm just a working bloke like yourselves – car mechanic actually. Now, any questions?' 'Yes,' said Tommy. 'Could you spare me a minute after the game... I think my fuel pump's gone.' Exit another flustered ref.

Ron Yeats, our team captain, was my closest mate at Anfield. When Shanks signed the big fellow from Dundee United he was so pleased he invited the local press corps to the club, took them into the dressing room and said: 'Walk round him lads... he's a Colossus!' Just after this well recorded occasion he bumped into the then Everton manager, the late Harry Catterick. Catterick enquired after the Yeats signing and Shanks, pleased as punch, at having got big Ron, told him: 'Yes Harry, I've got him, and I'll tell you what, with him at centre half I could play Arthur Askey in goal.'

Yeatsie, of course, didn't always meet with Shanks' approval. After one defeat Shanks, looking for an excuse, turned on the big man and asked what

he had called when he tossed the coin. 'Heads,' replied Ron. 'Come on man, surely you know you should have called tails!' growled Bill.

Gordon Milne was another who suffered at the hands of Shanks, albeit not intentionally. I remember in the early days, when we were still in the second division and playing Derby County at the Baseball Ground. I was new to the scene but Gordon, having been around for some time, knew everyone and at the end of the game lingered to chat to some of the Derby lads. Shanks, who hated waiting any longer than necessary after any game, gave his usual brief press conference and then jumped onto the coach and it was 'Wagons-Ho' back to Liverpool. Unfortunately Gordon was still chatting inside and was left stranded. We were back at Anfield before anyone noticed he was missing and by that time it was too late. One of England's best mid-field men was left to thumb a lift back home.

Peter Thompson, that marvellous winger who was to become part of England's successful World Cup winning squad in 1966, joined us from Preston and in the early days was having a nightmare time of it, possibly, we used to joke, because he wasn't used to the crowds. When things got serious Shanks pulled him in for a pep talk. 'Now son, you're not doing the business and there's got to be a reason... you're obviously drinking too much.' Peter, a quiet unassuming lad, countered: 'But boss I don't drink, just an occasional half pint after a game, but that's all.' 'Aye' said Shanks, thinking hard, 'so you're going with the women.' Peter, by this time trembling before the great man, answered: 'No boss I don't go with women – I've not even got a girl friend.' Shankly continued: 'Is it the night club's then? They're dens of iniquity them son.' Peter, by this time almost in tears, answered: 'Boss, honestly I don't know any nightclubs. I just stay in my digs and at the weekend go to the pictures.' Shanks, puzzled but never beaten, wound up the conversation: 'Aye, well I'll tell you something son... you've missed your vocation... you should have been a bloody monk!'

Billy Stevenson was the joker in the dressing

room, and Shanks lapped him up. 'A laughing dressing room is a winning dressing room' he would say. But there was one famous occasion when Stevo had Shanks laughing on the other side of his face – and the incident brought about another piece of Anfield policy that lived on. We were playing Manchester United and Stevenson, at a throw-in, threw the ball back to Ron Yeats. George Best, always alert, ran like an arrow at Ron, robbed him of the ball, ran on and stuck it in the net. After the match Shanks held a post mortem and decided there and then that Stevenson would never again throw to Ron Yeats, and that no Liverpool player would ever throw the ball back to his own centre-half. A simple piece of Shankly logic but again a good one. Stevenson, like Gerry Byrne, had became part of Liverpool folklore because of one error.

Ian Callaghan, that great little Liverpool and England winger, seldom gave Shankly any reason for anger. His behaviour on and off the field was exemplary but the halo slipped once when we were on a European trip to Belgium. As we arrived back at the hotel, having broken Shanks' curfew by having a few drinks too many at some club, we were all duly given a dressing down by the boss. This was something we were, in the main, fairly used to. Little Ian, stood swaying in the doorway as Shanks rounded on him last of all: 'And as for you Callaghan... you of all people... I'm going to tell your wife on you!'

My striking partner up front was, of course, the immaculate Roger Hunt. He was known as 'Sir Roger' to our fans and was a member of England's World Cup winning side of 1966. Roger and Geoff Strong were, and still are, great muckers, and while playing were avid card men. Not for a lot of money, but compulsive players of a game called 'hearts' which, like Rummy, gave you a points tally at the end of a session. And what sessions Hunt and Strong would have. I remember one European trip when the

● *The Liverpool team, 1965. Back row (left to right): Milne, Byrne, Lawrence, Yeats, Lawlor, Stevenson. Front row (left to right): Callaghan, Hunt, St John, Smith, Thompson.*

cards came out as we boarded the coach at Anfield. Play continued at the airport, on the plane, on the coach to the hotel, after dinner, after breakfast, after training etc. etc. The only time they did not play was on the coach to the game itself. And the whole procedure was repeated on the way home until they finally put the cards away back at Anfield. I remember them tallying up as we left for home – after three days of continuous play Roger owed Geoff ten pence!

Tommy Smith, Ron Yeats and Bobby Graham, a highly skilled little inside forward who later played for me at Motherwell, were the real card sharps – but only until they skinned Shanks! It happened on a trip to Newcastle. Shanks enjoyed a game of cards. He used to always remind us that in his home village of Glenbuck the miners used to play constantly after work, behind the dressing rooms of the local football club. 'And many a time I would go home to my mother with filthy crumpled up ten bob notes and say "iron them will you, I'm going out tonight".'

Anyway Shanks got himself involved in a game of blind three-card brag with Bobby Graham and some of the lads. Bobby was gong blind, which meant that Shanks had to pay double every time on his seen hand. As the players dropped out only Graham and Shanks, plus a fair pile of money, were left. Shanks eventually said: 'Bobby, I'll put you out of your misery son... three Jacks.' He went to scoop up the money. Graham then turned up his blind hand – three threes. 'I win' said Shanks. 'No you don't,' said Bobby. 'Three threes is tops in this school.' There then followed an enormous row. 'Three Jacks win in Chicago' claimed Shanks. In the end Smithy told him: 'Bobby's right boss... three threes win.' Shanks stormed off owing Bobby a few pounds. 'See me on Monday when we get home Graham,' he growled.

On Monday, Bobby took his courage in both hands and knocked on the guvnor's door. 'There's your money son... but no more cards. That gambling is bad for you,' ordered a peeved Shankly, 'cut it out.'

From then on the lads substituted match sticks for money and Shanks kept away.

4 TEAM-MATES – BY GREAVSIE

ike Ian I had the privilege of playing with a team which, even now, is recognised as one of the greatest club sides ever to grace British football. It was, of course, the Tottenham Hotspur side of the sixties. A team which offered fans class football and that most important of commodities, goals. People often include me in the side which won the League and Cup double in 1961. They're wrong, of course; in fact I didn't join Spurs until the year after, for that £99,999 fee I've spoken of in another chapter.

During my time at White Hart Lane I never won a League championship medal but I do have two FA Cup and one Cup Winners' Cup medal to show for nine marvellous years. Let me say right away it was a pleasure to play alongside so many great players. Ask any older Spurs fan to name that team and he will reel off Brown, Baker and Henry; Blanchflower, Norman and Mackay; Jones, White, Smith, Greaves and Dyson or Medwin. Les Allen was there too when Smithy was injured, and later there were Pat Jennings, Alan Gilzean and Cyril Knowles.

Every one of these players was a true professional, highly skilled, competitive, men you could trust in a crisis. And they were Tottenham Hotspur through and through. Often I think back on another Shanklyism – when asked his team before a match he would say: 'Same as last season.' Shankly was making the point that a settled team is the best team. And as usual he was right. The same could be said for our lot. Of course there were changes but they were minimal and Bill Nicholson, like Shankly, knew the value of putting the same eleven on the field week after week. It certainly worked for Spurs in my hey-day, I reckon we were just about the most exciting side in Britain in the early sixties (sorry Saint!) – we packed the ground at White Hart Lane in a way today's directors must envy.

But really it's down to entertainment and commitment. Sadly over the last few years Spurs have lost the ability to combine entertainment with the hardness needed to win trophies and championships. It's sad, but until the blend is right the fans will stay away. And no doubt the young Spurs fans will have to put up with their parents boring the pants off them about the 'good old days'. Mind you they were good old days. For not only could my White Hart Lane team-mates play a bit. Some of them, like me, did like their bit of fun too.

Scottish goalkeepers, as any of you who watch Saint and Greavsie will know, have often been the subject of, shall we say, some ribaldry from me. Recently Jim Leighton has spoiled my bit of fun. Young Jim is the steadiest keeper I've seen in a Scotland jersey for a long time. Scots will remind me of Ronnie Simpson and, of course, Old Ron did give a bit of stability for a few games before a bad shoulder injury forced him to give up at the grand old age of 40. But for my money the best Scottish keeper in the last 25 years was my old Spurs team-mate Bill Brown. Bill got the nickname Dracula from the rest of us – the old boy just didn't like crosses – but what a reflex keeper that man was. I've told elsewhere how Danny Blanchflower's pre-match pep-talk won us the European Cup Winners' Cup against Athletico Madrid in 1963. But the very fact that we made it to that Rotterdam final was thanks to Bill Brown... and a superlative display of goalkeeping against Slovan Bratislava.

We had to play the Czechs in mid-winter and they had a fine team, the nucleus of which actually played for Czechoslovakia in the 1962 World Cup Final against the great Brazil side. It had been such a hard winter in Czechoslovakia that the River Danube had frozen over. When we arrived in Bratislava we couldn't believe the pitch we had to play on. It was covered in ice with a thin covering of water – the thaw had finally set in! But play we had to, and when I say that Bill Brown must have had one hundred and fifty touches of the ball and the rest of us zero – that about sums up Bill's contribution and ours. Suffice to say that I have never seen a display of goalkeeping like it. Almost everything that the Czechs threw at Bill he saved. He had the all-time great Czech players such as Masupost and Popluhar holding their heads in amazement as he touched sure fire winners over the crossbar and round posts. The shots and headers kept on coming but Bill stood firm. In the end though he was beaten twice and we had a two goal deficit to take back to White Hart Lane in the second leg. That it wasn't 12–0 was down to Bill Brown.

I remember coming off at the end alongside Bobby Smith. The Czech keeper, one of the best in Europe, came up to shake Bobby Smith's hand. Smithy, always the gentleman, spurned the gesture and growled: 'Londres.' The poor keeper didn't know then what he meant – but he did a fortnight later! Bill Brown had done his bit in Bratislava it was up to us to repay him in London – and we did.

If Bill got it hot in Czechoslovakia, then Smith's goalkeeper friend had it boiling over in London. Within five minutes he had been hammered into the back of the net, complete with the ball, by his old pal Bobby and from then on didn't want to know. We won 6–0 on the night, 6–2 on aggregate. Our full backs were Peter Baker and Ron Henry. Peter, now in South Africa, was a good solid player. Ron Henry got one cap for England and to my mind should have had many more. An underrated left-back, he once

● *Tottenham, 1961. League Champions and winners of the F.A. Cup, Spurs parade in all their glory, but I didn't join until the following year. Back row (left to right): Brown, Baker, Henry, Blanchflower, Norman, Mackay. Front row (left to right): Jones, White, Smith, Allen, Dyson. The League Cup is the one on the left*

turned the tables on a typical John White gag when we were in Europe, leaving Whitey not such a pretty boy.

Ron is a market gardener now and doing very well I believe. In his playing days he was a budgie-fancier and John White, an irrepressible character, was always chirping at him about his hobby. But one night in Europe he went too far.

We were all sitting round a table waiting for dinner when a waiter approached Ron (a man not over-endowed with humour) holding a platter with a massive silver cover. When Ron lifted the cover there on the plate was, not a steak, but what looked like half a ton of budgie seed. While we convulsed with laughter Ron, who didn't see the joke, threw the whole thing up in the air. We were all covered from head to foot in the Yugoslavian equivalent of Trill. It was steak and budgie seed for us.

Then there was Danny. The loveable Irishman with a twinkle in his eye and a brain in his head which left all of us, including the Tottenham board at the time, standing. Danny Blanchflower was a highly intelligent, highly articulate leader whom I believe would have been worth a fortune in today's game. He could handle himself superbly with players, managers, directors and fans and was an expert reader of a game of football. Many a game we snatched from the jaws of defeat due to Danny Blanchflower's natural intuition. He was, of course, Bill Nicholson's strong right arm, the guvnor on the field, and he was before his time in tactical planning.

It's not generally known that Blanchflower was the man who introduced the defensive wall to football. It happened when he was part of the Northern Ireland squad which did so well in the 1958 World Cup. The Irish, against all the odds, got to Sweden and with clever players such as Blanchflower, Peter McFarland, Jimmy McIlroy, Peter Doherty and Billy Bingham in their line-up they proved no pushovers. In fact they went out in the quarter-final stages but not before they had sparked off a sight which was to become commonplace – the defensive wall at free kicks just outside the box.

In those days the last line of defence at free kicks was a bit haphazard... one player marking his opposite number. Danny and McIlroy perfected the wall system to such an extent that the Irish only went out in the end to France, beaten 4–0 in the quarter-finals mainly due to injuries to key players.

If Danny Blanchflower was the thinker in the Spurs team then centre half Maurice Norman was our Colossus. Big Norm was 6ft 4ins of solid muscle, a white Frank Bruno whose job on the field was to win the ball with head and feet and then smack it up to the forwards. Off the field Maurice was a quiet man. On the field he was a terror – he certainly frightened the life out of opposing forwards. He won 23 caps for England and deservedly so. When people talk about stopper centre halves then he was the model. He wasn't a frilly player but he sure was effective.

Next to Maurice we had Dave Mackay, the hunk of Scots granite whom I believe was Tottenham Hotspur's greatest-ever player. Mackay to me had everything. He was the perfect wing half, iron hard, dynamic, creative, skilful and a natural leader of men. Dave took over the Spurs captaincy from Danny and inspired everyone around him. The man was pure magic and the fans loved him. I can see him now marshalling the defence, roaring commands, tackling like a steel trap, surging forward, that great chest thrust out, and finally placing a perfect ball at the feet of Cliff Jones, Bobby Smith or myself. What other player could come back from two broken legs and still be as good as ever?

I was asked recently what two players I would choose if I was a manager today and could have my pick of past and present. One would be Dave Mackay – the other George Best. Both were greats. There can be no other description of them. And if Mackay was an inspiration on the field then he was a good companion off.

Dave, like myself, was not averse to the occasional lager and we had many a session after an important game. The strange thing about Dave was that he was always able to train harder than anyone else the next day. He played hard both on and off the field but he could also put in hard work like there was no

tomorrow. In fact I can honestly say I only saw Dave Mackay play one bad game for Spurs, and that was on a summer trip to Israel and after a typical night on the local nectar.

We were due to play Haifa the next day and Mackay and I decided that the opposition was such that victory was assured and a drinking session would not affect our chances. As the evening wore on our trainer Cecil Poynton kept reminding us that we would be playing in temperatures of ninety degrees the next day, but he was consoled by our outright lies that we had only had a couple of beers. Truth be told we had more than a dozen and all of us were slipping the empties behind massive drapes in the hotel lounge. When bedtime finally arrived we staggerd out into the main hall to be confronted by Cecil who was turning the air blue with expletives. For there nestling behind the drapes but in full view of everyone passing through were about a hundred empty lager bottles. And so to bed!

The next day was a memorable one. It was the only time I ever heard Dave Mackay complain of feeling rough after a night out. As we took the field our skipper looked a little worse for wear but every-thing seemed normal as he killed a ball on his chest, controlled it with the knee and coolly swept the ball back to Bill Brown. Brown, who had been drinking snowballs the night before (imagine a Scot drinking snowballs!) could only watch as the Israeli centre forward said 'Thank you very much' and smacked the ball home. One down in thirty seconds and the great man Mackay hung his head in shame. Cecil Poynton shook his head in a knowing way and the rest of us knew we had to do something quick. We did. We went on to win 4–1 but Mackay never lived that one down.

Dave was, like his fellow Scot the late, great John White, a practical joker, and often he would have Terry Dyson or Terry Medwin tearing their hair out with his pranks. One of his favourite ploys was to get hold of a team-mate's complimentary tickets and kindly leave them in an envelope – but not before he had ripped them into a thousand pieces! The 'boots out the window' trick was another favourite jest of our skipper. Many a coach driver had to put the brakes on sharpish as the cry would go up: 'Dyson's boots are away'. Dave had done his hammer thrower's act with Terry's size 5's. Little Terry used to have to scamper from the coach and, red-faced, retrieve the footwear as Bill Nicholson gave him an earful. Strange it was never Mackay who got the blame – such was his influence on the team, and the boss! All these pranks were taken in good humour. It did help to have a laugh on tours abroad, and White and Mackay kept us as merry as the whisky which bears their names as the miles sped by.

The pair were also two of the big card players in the Spurs camp and, like Roger Hunt and Geoff Strong with Liverpool, their card schools would go on throughout Europe. I remember once a train we were travelling on stopped for ten minutes and I got out with the rest of the lads to stretch my legs. After a while I realised that Mackay, White and Dyson were missing and I started looking for them. I eventually found them still playing cards – on a tombstone in a cemetery – behind the station. They had played all the way from London across Europe and couldn't leave the cards down for a minute!

Our two wingers consisted of the Welsh wizard Cliff Jones on the right, and little Terry Dyson on the left. Jones was a world-class footballer. Dyson, along with Peter Baker, was the only Spurs player in our side not to be capped. Terry was like a little boy lost when it came to home international time. The rest of us were off playing for England, Scotland, Ireland or Wales while he was left at White Hart Lane. Yet he had something I only wish some players of today would copy, the ability to play to limited strengths. Don't get me wrong. Terry was a good little professional. He was speedy, could move into space, fire in dangerous crosses and take a goal with the best of them. But he never attempted to be something he wasn't. So often today I feel like tearing what's left of my hair out when I see a kid come into a team because, say, of his ability to run at defences. And then because of a little bit of press praise he attempts to become a George Best. It will never happen and as soon as he learns to play to his own strengths he'll be a much better player. Dyson was like that. He put his pace and crossing ability to great use, and he finished up winning League and Cup double medals and scoring twice in the Cup Winners' Cup Final.

Terry was also my room-mate for quite a time and he had one other great ability – he could read a paperback in two hours flat. Often I would toss and turn as he kept the light on to speed read his way through a book. After his umpteenth fag – he was also a chain smoker – the light would go out and I would say: 'Finished are we Terry?' 'Yes Jim, I've read it all.' 'Thank goodness for that' I would moan, 'maybe I can get some sleep now.'

Jonesy on the right wing was something else. He could take a man on the run inside or out – and boy could he run. He was also one of the greatest headers of a ball I've ever seen. He was a small man and, sparing his blushes, like the Saint was springheeled. He could jump above the tallest of defenders. And he could score goals too. Often I look back on that forward line and think of the goals we used to put away. Bobby Smith and I notched around 65 a season between us, Cliff Jones could always be guaranteed to grab around twenty, Terry Dyson always managed fifteen or sixteen as did John White. Add to that Dave Mackay's occasional blockbuster and we were totalling over 100 goals per season. Little wonder we were hard to beat.

The strange thing about Cliff was that he never really got the wage he deserved at Tottenham. He was always amongst the more poorly paid and in fact, since he and I were roughly the same size, I used to give him my old England suits. Imagine Wales' top player walking about in an England suit. It sounds hilarious now, but at the time we didn't think much about it. I never fancied the England tailor's work anyway. In those days I was a snappy dresser and, since I reckoned the England smutter was the work of some blind seamster, Jonesy got quite a few cast-offs. Mind you, on one occasion – again abroad – I could have murdered Cliff.

As I said, in those days I liked the smart gear – the best of jackets, ties, shirts and shoes. I recall on one trip I was rooming with Cliff. I had bought myself a pair of sandals for the beach, leaving a brand new pair of expensive crocodile shoes in the room. After a while on the sand, I turned round to see Cliff plodding towards me scuffing the sand as he went – in my lovely new shoes! I have been known to utter a curse or two when annoyed and that day the air was bluer than the sea!

Cliff was a great family man. He and his wife Joanie have five lovely kids, but in those days the club took advantage of him. He was never one to cause a fuss, but after one Welsh tour of South America where he outshone members of the great Brazilian team which included such as Pele, Gerson and Jairzinho, he decided to take a stand. He told us he was going to have it out with Bill Nicholson once and for all. He was fed up being skint and was going to ask for £100 per week. Now since I was the first Spurs man on £100 per week, and that didn't happen until a year or two later, Cliff was backing a loser. We all knew it, and players being players we all waited in the White Hart across the road from the ground for Cliff to regale us with tales of revolution. It was all too obvious from Cliff's face that things hadn't gone to plan with the great white chief. After a couple of pints the story came out.

'I went straight in you know,' said Cliff. 'The boss was behind that big desk as usual and I told him "you've seen the papers, I want a hundred pounds a week… I'm one of the World's best players!"' At this Bill Nicholson fixed him with that ice cold stare of his and said: 'That might be your opinion son, it's not mine.' Exit Jonesy into the unsympathetic arms of his Spurs mates – all doubled up with laughter. Still, I'll say this, Cliff *was* worth £100 a week – he was brilliant.

One of my big mates, and I do mean big, was Bobby Smith our centre-forward. A tank of a man he smashed his way through the best of defences and into the England team alongside me. We had a fine partnership for both club and country but Bobby had one problem in those days, he was a gambler. Now I know many a good footballer has fallen foul of the bookie – some irretrievably – it's the way of life

41

I suppose. You have time on your hands in the afternoons and, if you're not a golfer, then where better to spend it than on a racecourse.

I like a bet, a small one, but in those days I hardly bothered at all. Bobby made up for me. He was always ducking and diving to have a bet and more often than not he'd wind up skint. On one spectacular occasion I actually paid for his Spanish holiday – and even now I can only laugh at it.

It happened in 1962. We had had a good run. We won the F.A. Cup, made the European Cup semi-finals and had played a few times for England. Plenty of bonus money around so when Bobby and his missus, plus my wife Irene and myself, booked a holiday in Torremolinos it seemed a bumper time was to be had by all. But the wheels of our Viscount had only just lifted from the runway at Heathrow when Bobby broke the bad news: 'Jim, I'm skint. Don't tell the wife.'

I couldn't believe it. Here we were going on a joint holiday and Bobby hadn't a peseta to call his own. The horses, it seems, hadn't been running too well and Bobby, the iron man of English football, was afraid to break the news to his nearest and dearest. I had around £200 with me, a lot of money in those days, so I split the cash with Bobby and we plotted to get a few quid more.

'It's easy,' said the bold Bob. 'We've our bonus money from the Cup Final, and England appearances, due at Spurs. We'll get the club to wire it all out here, I can pay you back the cash you gave me and have plenty to spare. Don't worry.' I wasn't worried either, until two days after when we arrived at Thomas Cook's to collect our wads. 'Meester Greaves,' shouted the teller. I went forward, signed on the dotted line and out thumped £300 worth of pesetas – my back pocket was bulging. Then it was Smithy's turn. But 'Meester Smith' only got a few hundred pesetas – around a fiver's worth in fact. 'The buggers!' shouted Bobby. 'They've obviously taken my Cup Final tickets money off what I was due. Sorry Jim, but could I borrow another hundred and

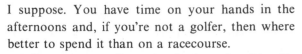

● *F.A. Cup Final, 1962: Spurs v. Burnley. Bobby Smith scores the second goal while I look on*

43

fifty?'

What could I do? I gave Bobby another wedge and then spent my fortnight's holiday gritting my teeth as Mavis, Bobby's missus, went round buying up what seemed to me the whole of Torremolinos. I returned home a poorer but wiser man. Needless to say I never saw the money again.

Going to the races with Smithy was quite an occasion. I remember Spurs going as guests to the Caister Holiday Camp at Yarmouth and Bobby was never out of the bookies. That week the horses were running as fast as Cliff Jones and towards the end of the week the local bookmaker put the bar on Bobby. Smithy had won nearly four hundred quid and the poor sod couldn't afford to let him bet any more. He was daft though. Bobby took the whole lot round to Yarmouth racetrack and blew every last penny. I had to lend him a tenner to get home!

On another occasion in South Africa we agreed to put fifty rand in the kitty each – Bobby would do the betting and I would be the banker. We were going like bombs on the eight race card – up around 400 rand (£300) going into the last race. I knew that post-time was danger time and searched desperately for Bobby in the crowds. I tell you I never moved as fast in any penalty area as I did that day, but I still never got to Bob in time. My worst fears were realised when I saw him sitting dejected amongst the discarded tickets – he had blown the lot in the last. Bus fare home time again!

After Smithy, my next bosom – or should I say boozing – buddy at Spurs was Alan Gilzean. Alan was signed under tragic circumstances. John White had died after being struck by lightning on a golf course and a special Scotland versus England testimonial was held at White Hart Lane for his dependents. Alan came, played well, and Bill Nicholson signed him.

Alan hailed from Couper Angus. I used to joke with him that he came from a cave there, but there was nothing primitive about his play. He looked an unlikely footballer but he had earned a great reputation with Dundee and Scotland and he was to be a White Hart Lane hero, for me as well as the fans.

He was great in the air and I fed off his little flicked headers and subtle passes to score a barrow full of goals. Gillie was more than just a header of the ball. He was good too on the ground. His pace was deceptive and he could shimmy through a defence as easy as pie. A great player and a pleasure to play alongside. He was also a drinker – just the man to partner Greavsie off the field as well as on!

Alan, like myself, was not much of a trainer. Don't get me wrong, Gillie could run alright. In fact I've rarely met someone with his stamina but he was like me, a bit lazy – and that used to annoy our coach, Eddie Baily, and the boss. We soon learned that the quickest way to get a drink after training was to keep the gaffer's tactics talks down to a minimum. So before we went in to any meeting, we would browbeat everyone into not asking questions. That way pub time came a lot sooner.

Actually in those days we didn't need any long tactics talks anyway. We had a great team, and frankly we didn't give a damn about opposing teams. We felt we could beat them all. Anyway, Bill Nicholson would ramble on and then ask: 'Any questions?' Gillie and I, sitting at the back, would have the heads down willing everyone to keep stum. At first it worked then Bill Nick, the wily old fox, sussed what was going on. After five minutes silence he would point the finger at Alan and I and shout: 'You two bastards have got to them again!' Guilty as charged!

Two youngsters who were to become part and parcel of the scene at White Hart Lane joined us on the same day – Cyril Knowles and Pat Jennings. It's amazing to think that Big Pat has only just called it a day after his World Cup trip to Mexico with Northern Ireland while the rest of us, including Cyril, have long since retired. And I'll let you into a secret. Big Pat, like Gillie and I, was a little loathe to take training seriously in the early days. He was quick enough. In fact I reckon when he was in the mood, Pat Jennings was the quickest player on the Spurs staff. In fact Pat enjoyed playing out in practice. He used to play up front and I used to get my chance in goal. Mind you, I wasn't too hot with

the high crosses!

I got an early introduction to Pat's bravery in a six-a-side match at the end of training one day, indoors for a change. Pat was in the opposition goal when I was sent clear. I sold him a lovely dummy – the only problem was he didn't buy it! I woke up ten minutes later in the dressing room. I needed five stitches after we had clashed head on. Pat had an egg on his forehead too, but being Irish he hadn't felt the collision like I had.

Pat was one of the greatest professionals I ever played with. His longevity as a goalkeeper at international level proves he was one of the greatest ever. A credit to Spurs, to football and to goalkeeping.

As I've mentioned, to play for Spurs in those days was to mean an almost automatic call up from your country. Cyril Knowles was to prove himself a fine Spurs and England full back, and, of course, he eventually got a song to himself at White Hart Lane – the unforgettable 'Nice One Cyril'. I used to kid him that it should have been Danny Kaye's 'Ugly Duckling' that should have been his theme tune. That was all down to his first few weeks with us at Spurs. Every pre-season we had a series of cricket matches against local club sides and being a cricket nut I used to organise the team. I was duly doing the rounds when young Cyril came up and told me: 'Put me down as opening bat Greavsie. I come from the same village as Geoff Boycott . . . you'll not get better than me.' Suitably impressed, I put Cyril in first in our opening match and then watched as he was clean bowled middle stump first ball. Exit a red-faced Cyril with the rest of us doubled up. To be fair Cyril turned out to be an excellent cricketer in later matches – but the boys never let him forget his debut.

I loved my nine years at Spurs. I had wonderful companions, some fantastic moments and an abundance of good times. The fans were superb and if it was me who got the goals every other player deserved credit for them too. I was in paradise. What striker could fail with the back-up I had. Naturally I have my favourite memories but winning the three cup medals – two FA Cup and one Cup Winners'

Cup – have got to take pride of place.

The Cup Winners' Cup Final against Atletico Madrid will always stand out. Not just because I scored two goals in our 5–1 victory but because on that May night we became the first ever British club to win a European trophy. It was an experience I'll never forget. It seemed half of London was there to cheer us on. And after the Blanchflower pep-talk I've spoken of elsewhere we were unstoppable – particularly Terry Dyson. It was Terry's night of nights. After only fifteen minutes he provided me with a picture cross for me to prod us ahead. Just after the half-hour Terry scored himself to put us 2–0 up. And it was my little room-mate who got us out of trouble in the second half after the Spaniards had gone one back through a penalty.

We were battling a bit when Terry swung over a high swirling cross. The Spanish keeper mis-timed his leap and the ball was in the back of the net. We were 3–1 up and no-one was going to stop us then. Dyson, what a match he had, swept over another cross ten minutes from the end which I got on the end of to make 4–1, and for his finale little Terry ran 30 yards before hammering home a fifth from all of 25 yards. It was a fantastic performance from the little man and, as we trooped off the field to get our medals, Bobby Smith ruffled his hair and said: 'Terry, you can retire now. You'll never play better.'

My first taste of winning a Wembley Cup Final came in 1962 when Spurs successfully defended the trophy which had won them the double the previous year. Actually Burnley, who had a fine side, were fancied a bit to beat us in that Final but after I put us ahead early on and then Bobby Smith scored as good a goal as you'll see at Wembley to put us 2–0 up we were never in much danger. Jim Robson did pull one back for Burnley but Danny Blanchflower wrapped it all up in typically cool manner by slotting home a penalty goal late on. It was around this time that the Glory days were born. The fans singing their heads off with that marvellous 'Glory Glory Tottenham Hotspur' anthem which was to resound around grounds – a wall of sound which helped us feel unbeatable.

I was to get back to another FA Cup Final with Spurs. This was in 1967 when we met Chelsea in the first all-London final. Actually the whole thing was a bit of an anti-climax following the press build-up. Bill Nicholson had rebuilt the great side of the early sixties but with Mackay as skipper we feared no-one. It has to be said though that dear old Ron 'Chopper' Harris kept me fairly quiet throughout. On the day that didn't matter too much. We were far too good for Chelsea.

It's funny how little omens occurred before some of our big cup victories. There was the famous Blanchflower pep-talk in Rotterdam, and in the 1967 Final we got a morning morale boost when some of the Chelsea youngsters seemed nervous when interviewed for television. It was one of the first finals television covered in a big way and it certainly worked to our advantage.

Jimmy Robertson scored a fine goal to put us one up at the break and half-way through the second half Frank Saul, with his back to the Chelsea goal, swivelled to connect with a Mackay throw-in and Peter Bonnetti was caught completely by surprise – two-nil! Bobby Tambling did get one back for the Blues near the end but we held on comfortably to hear the 'Glory Glory' chants ringing round Wembley again – marvellous moments, moments no footballer ever forgets.

In my days at Spurs I had only two regrets – that I never won a Championship medal and that the club never won the European Cup. Certainly our team in the early sixties was good enough to win a European Cup. That we didn't I believe was down to three of the worst decisions I've ever seen by referees and all in the one tie. In Spurs' European Cup run of season 1961–62 I was not eligible for selection until the semi-final stages when we drew the holders Benfica. The first game in Lisbon proved to be crucial. The Portuguese had a fine side and beat us 3–1 before their own fans – but to my mind we should have

● *F.A. Cup Final, 1967: Tottenham v. Chelsea.*
Bonnetti lets in the first goal scored by Robertson.
Venables is alongside me in the picture
Inset: Dave Mackay clears the ball from the oncoming Tambling

48

drawn 3–3

The referee was Swiss and I couldn't believe it when I scored a perfectly good goal only to be called off-side. It was a ridiculous decision. I had actually beaten the full-back before sliding the ball home. But worse was to come near the end. I took the ball to the goal-line and pulled it back for Bobby Smith to smash it home. It was a fine goal but again the referee ruled it out for off-side. That would have made it 3–2 and, in the end, that would have been enough but instead we got back to White Hart Lane before a capacity crowd a fortnight later and quickly found ourselves 4–1 down on aggregate. Aguas, a fine player, who had scored in the first leg, combined with Simoes to slip the ball past Bill Brown. Again we lost out on a controversial refereeing decision. This time the Danish referee who, to my mind, had been brow-beaten by the wily Benfica boss Bela Guttman with stories in the press about the rough-tough Spurs pair Smith and Mackay ruled out yet another of my efforts after good work by John White and big Bobby. Again I am convinced the goal should have stood – that it didn't cost us dearly.

We hit the Portuguese as hard as we knew how. Smithy finally did get a goal on the board and when Danny Blanchflower slotted home a penalty with only five minutes of the second half gone the crowd rose to us as never before. To say the Benfica goal had a charmed life was the biggest understatement in football. I'm a great believer that if the gods are not with you then you have no chance. Following the disallowing of those three earlier goals, it seemed that no matter what we did we were not going to get the breakthrough goal. We absolutely pulverised the Benfica goal but Costa Pereira had several instinctive reflex saves and we also hit the woodwork three times. Our last fling, as I remember, was a Mackay effort that smashed back off a sodden crossbar. It was a frantic fantastic second-half played throughout in drenching rain. But in the end it was Benfica who hung on to go through to play Real Madrid in the Final. We had lost the tie 4–3.

I remember Bill Nicholson saying at the time that he felt that if we could beat the Portuguese then we could beat Real in the Final. He was probably right. Benfica went on to win one of the greatest ever European Cup Finals beating the great Spaniards 5–3 in Amsterdam. A year later in Holland we were to have our European night of glory... but the disappointment of that unlucky rainy evening against Benfica still rankles.

I've left the saddest memory of my Spurs teammates to last – the John White tragedy when our talented Scottish inside-forward was struck down and killed by lightning on a golf course. Whitey, as I've said, was a prankster and a real character. He was also a great little inside man in the true Scottish mould.

He was christened 'The Ghost' and that description fitted John perfectly. On the park he was always ghosting into the right position. When you looked up he always seemed to be in space and had he lived I'm sure he would have gone into the history books as one of the all-time Scottish greats. He was certainly one of my all-time favourite players.

His death was a major blow to everyone who knew him, and strangely to us all at Tottenham, like the Kennedy assasination, everyone could remember exactly where they were when the news broke.

I remember the day well. The weather was diabolical. Monsoon rains sweeping London and the Home Counties, skies black with thunder clouds. I had been at a business lunch with my brother-in-law, who was then my business partner, and our bank manager. The conditions were so bad that when we returned to his bank in Tottenham the place was flooded. When I got home I got a 'phone call to say 'Whitey's dead'. I thought at first it was a false alarm – in later years I was involved in one myself – but it was true. I was stunned and I had lost a great friend.

The real tragedy, we were told later, was that John's death might just have been avoided had someone been with him. John had gone out to play golf by himself. There was a downpour and he sheltered under a tree. The lightning struck and he lay for almost half an hour before he was discovered. By that time it was too late. Medical people told us later that had someone been with him to shake him or give him the kiss of life then he might have lived. As it was football had lost a great little personality.

Ian too remembers John White.

Like Jimmy I lost a friend, and Scotland a great player, in Johnny White. We made our international debuts together for Scotland and I remember nodding the ball down for Whitey to score his first international goal – against West Germany. And like Jimmy the day he died will be etched in my memory forever. I was in hospital recovering from peritonitis. I had almost died myself with the illness, when the news came through. I couldn't believe that the lad I enjoyed as player and companion had gone. I later played in his memorial match at White Hart Lane and I don't believe there was a dry eye anywhere.

Most of John's mates have a favourite story about his pranks. Mine happened during a Scotland training session. Dave Mackay had one favourite trick – tearing up players complimentary tickets. One day John caught his Spurs skipper napping. A Scots official had handed out the complimentaries to everyone – but Mackay was missing. When Dave came to our table he spied the white envelope containing tickets in John's place at the dinner table. As John approached Dave ripped the envelope into little pieces completely destroying the tickets. Laughing, he said to Whitey: 'Are those yours John?' Cool as a cucumber John pulled his tickets out and said: 'No Dave... I've got mine safe and sound.' Pointing to the tiny pieces of paper in front of him told Mackay: 'I reckon that's what's left of yours!'

The Scotland camp erupted with laughter. Mackay had been caught at his own game. Whitey had outwitted him.

5 ENGLAND, THE WORLD CUP AND JIMMY GREAVES

The World Cup. The very mention of the event is enough to turn footballers knees, and managers minds, to jelly. To me the World Cup is the greatest sporting tournament. The Olympics are great, the Superbowl may be magnificent, but it is the World Cup that reaches the places and people other events do not. New heroes are born, old villains are resurrected. Third World countries emerge as footballing nations in an event that, with television coverage at saturation point, is beamed to the four corners of the World. Peasants and popes, communists and capitalists are hooked on the greatest sporting show on earth. The arguments from Mexico will, as ever, endure not only until 1990, but well beyond as well. The World Cup cannot be equalled in spectacle, interest, athleticism or skill. Try as they might, the Olympics, the Superbowl and the others, come a poor sporting second in most people's eyes.

IN THE BEGINNING — CHILE

World Cups, as you've gathered, have a special place in my life but perhaps not for the reasons you might imagine. My first taste of World Cup football was in 1962. I remember Chile for two reasons. I almost watched an England team-mate die, and I became famous as the man who discovered Garrincha's dog!

It was four years later that England won the World Cup at Wembley. Unfortunately it was also the year I lost out on a winners medal. Mind you I did have one consolation, I took a right few bob off the gentlemen of the press!

Mexico 1970! I was there as England suffered in the sun – but I got there the hard way – by car!

Certainly these World Cups have proved to be milestones in my life. Some of the experiences have been good, some bad, and some simply disastrous, but I suppose in a way I'm richer for them. They certainly would never have happened if I had not been a fairly famous footballer in the first place. The ordinary fan gets no chance to taste life like I did, more's the pity.

In the beginning there was Chile. For me the 1962

Finals were the forgotten World Cup, yet they produced the team I think was the greatest World Cup side ever, the Brazilian team which included stars such as Didi, Vava, Djalmar and Milton Santos, Amarildo and Garrincha. It's amazing to think that they actually walked away with the tournament without the great man Pele himself. Unfortunately there wasn't the same mass press and TV coverage as today so, while those great Brazilians were feted as soccer gods in their own country, they never made the same impact on the rest of the World as the Brazil team of 1970.

As for England, we had a fine young team back in 1962 and before the finals we had to fancy ourselves a bit. After all we had given quite a few good sides a hiding over the previous two years including one rather special 9–3 smashing of Scotland at Wembley which I somehow never fail to remind the old Saint about! But when we arrived in Chile after a short tour of America we had gone over the top a little. By the time it was all over we were absolutely shattered – both physically and mentally.

I've got to laugh nowadays when England squads complain about heat, accommodation, bad playing surfaces etc. Quite frankly they don't know they're born. I'd love to see them contending with the conditions we suffered in 1962.

Walter Winterbottom was manager and in the

● *The England World Cup Squad, 1962. Back row (left to right): Armfield, Robson, W. Winterbottom (manager), Flowers, Norman, Howe, Anderson, J. Adamson (coach), Shepherdson (trainer), Douglas. Front row (left to right): Connelly, Greaves, Swan, Hitchens, Springett, Haynes (captain), Hodgkinson, Wilson, Charlton, Peacock, Moore, Eastham, Hunt*

qualifying round we were drawn against Hungary, Argentina and Bulgaria. We were based in a spot which made Huddersfield look like Monte Carlo, a place called Rancagua which was a carbon copy of all those little Mexican towns 'the man with no name' used to ride into. It was cowboy country and one expected to bump into Clint Eastwood on every corner. The accommodation consisted of a litter of tin shacks surrounding the football pitch of a copper camp. And all this was 8,000 feet up in the mountains.

I was rooming with Bobby Moore and many a miserable day and night we spent, listening to the monsoon rain clattering against the corrugated iron roof of our hut. We had only one piece of light relief during the two weeks of our pre-match build-up. It was a 'dry' area which didn't please people such as Mooro and myself who were known to enjoy an occasional beer. So when Walter Winterbottom announced that the camp president was holding a reception in a Golf Club a few miles up the mountain and we were all invited, we were off like a shot. Once off the leash the lads were in no mood to return promptly to their life of boredom in the billet. The evening wore on and a few hours into the party Winterbottom sent the steady, sober figure of Jimmy Adamson to coax us back. When Jim arrived he was quickly conned into having a refreshing beer, then another, then another. It was well into the early hours before our coach returned, rather unsteadily, to base with a worried Walter standing at the front door. His face was a picture when he peered through the beery singing faces to see the untaintable Jimmy leading the choir from the back of the bus! Poor Jimmy, he's never been able to live that down with any of us who were there.

That was a rare bit of fun, but on the same trip we almost had a tragedy on our hands with an incident which, in retrospect, could have turned into the biggest disaster ever to hit a touring England party. As we trained in our hell-hole in the hills our centre half, Peter Swann of Sheffield Wednesday, took ill and was ordered to bed by trainer Harold Shepperson. It was in the days when we travelled without a

doctor and a type of 'flu was diagnosed.

Peter was rooming, I believe, with Gerry Hitchens and Alan Hodgkinson and of course, after training, we were all dropping in to see the big fellow. After a few days it occurred to us that the weight was beginning to drop off him. He began to look skeletal and suddenly the alarm bells were ringing. Peter was whisked to hospital where dysentry was diagnosed and he remained in bed for the rest of the trip. He was lucky he didn't die. He was so badly dehydrated that he was put on a drip immediately he was wheeled into the hospital. A few more days and he would have been a goner. The amazing thing is neither his room-mates, Hitchens, Hodgkinson, or anyone else in the camp, contracted the disease yet we were all regular visitors at his bedside. Needless to say after that scare we never travelled without a doctor again.

As you might imagine all this drama, coupled with the boredom, didn't exactly have us in the correct frame of mind for our opening match against Hungary. We lost 2–0.

In the second match we beat Argentina comfortably enough, 3–1. Then we met Bulgaria in what my old team-mate Bobby Charlton has since described as 'the worst game of football ever played' – a statement with which I wholeheartedly agree! We needed only a draw to qualify for the quarter-finals. Hungary had won the group before the Bulgaria match and to finish runners-up and gain the doubtful privilege of meeting the great Brazil in the quarter-finals, all we had to do was share the points with the Bulgars. Neither team came out of their own half. There was not a shot at goal and a sorry affair ended predictably 0–0. The only good thing about the match was that it was watched by possibly the poorest World Cup Final's crowd ever – around 1,500 poor suffering souls.

The Bulgarians? They were the lucky ones as they were going home. We moved into Vasco Da Gama to face Vava and company yearning not for glory but the airplane back to England. But it was in Vasco Da Gama I became a World Cup hero – of Brazil that is.

The Brazilians, who were always going to win the

World Cup anyway, duly gave us our soccer lesson and led us 3–1 mid-way through the second half. 'Not a bad result', I mused as play broke down in midfield. It was then my big moment came. Onto the field raced a mangy mongrel dog and, when the referee stopped play, some of my team-mates performed their best moves of the day to try to catch him. The whole thing became a bit of a circus until I was persuaded to lend a hand. I got down on my knees and, being a bit of a dog lover, managed to coax the cur to me. I grabbed it to the roars of an appreciative crowd but not, it appeared, to the appreciation of the mutt itself. A wet yellow patch suddenly appeared on my nice white England jersey – the ungrateful bugger had peed all over me! I moved quicker than I had all game and handed the hound to a security man, happy to rid myself of it. Little did I know that in one arresting moment I had become a superstar in soccer-mad Brazil.

The game duly finished 3–1 and we players were

on our way home to England for a holiday. Walter Winterbottom incidentally, was heading for the sack. But when the plane stopped off to refuel in Rio I got the surprise of my life. As we got out of the plane to stretch our legs a mass of fifty or so photographers were at the bottom of the steps. 'Where ees Meester Greeve?' they demanded. As the England lads pointed me out the flashbulbs popped. I was a hero and, until one of the English based reporters found out, I didn't know why. It appeared that Garrincha, that great little Brazilian winger, had taken a shiner to the mongrel who had so happily peed all over me. When we had left the Stadium he claimed the dog for his own and sent it back to his home in Brazil to join the rest of his menagerie. The Brazilian paparazzi getting wind of the story went crazy and I was front page news in football's maddest country. Mind you, I still pity the man I swapped jerseys with at the end of that game!

1966 AND ALL THAT

If 1962 in Chile was a disaster then 1966 in England was a delight. It was the swinging sixties, the Beatles, the mini-skirt, the year England won the World Cup – the year Greavsie missed out on the biggest day in English soccer history! Now of course I regret missing out on an historic occasion – but twenty years on it's time to put the record straight. I never was, never have been, never will be bitter at Alf Ramsey for leaving me out of the Final. Twenty years is a long time and over that period tales of rancour between Alf and myself have become legend – at least in the minds of football folk. But I'll tell you what, the stories shouldn't be classed as legend but as myth!

The stories have grown like the old first World War fable of a colonel who, sent the message down the line 'send reinforcements'. By the time it reached the General it had been translated as 'send three and fourpence'! I've heard them all. How I fell out with Alf because I wouldn't conform to his system; that I

● *World Cup Final, 1966. I can hardly believe it as I watch Geoff Hurst score the fourth goal and complete his hat-trick*

was dropped and never spoke to Ramsey again; that I hate Geoff Hurst because he got my place and became the first man to score a World Cup Final hat-trick. All a load of rot!

For the umpteenth and final time, I never quibbled with Ramsey's 'no wingers' policy. In fact I adapted easier than anyone. I got used to playing up front with only one other attacker in Italy.

I got on well with Ramsey and, most important of all, I wasn't *dropped* from the team.

The truth is I suffered a very bad shin gash (the marks of which I have to this day) had three stitches put in the wound after we beat France 2–0. Having been asked by Alf if I felt fit enough to face the Argentinians he later branded as 'animals', I truthfully had to answer 'no'. The rest is football history. Geoff played well against Portugal in the 2–1 semi-final win and Alf elected to say 'same again'

for the Final. And why not? The lads had played marvellously well against the Portuguese – Eusebio and all – and deserved the right to represent their country on it's greatest day. I might have been considered the best goal scorer in the squad but I had no divine right to a World Cup Final place. No, the aggro is all in the minds of fans and football people who do not know the inside story – and as for hating Geoff Hurst – what stuff and nonsense! No-one cheered louder than I when he scored his hat-trick – and people are wrong when they think I came away from the World Cup Final peeved and empty handed. Peeved perhaps that I had missed out on an historic occasion, but certainly not empty handed! I knew I would be collecting a few bob at the expense of some of the gentlemen of the press.

I had a few substantial bets with several of the members of the fourth estate when they mocked Alf

● *Having a friendly drink and chat with Sean Connery, Yul Brynner and Bobby Moore*

Ramsey's pre-tournament statement that England would win the World Cup.

I thoroughly agreed with him for two reasons. We had a damn good team and we were playing every match at home. And let's face it – how often do England lose at Wembley? (OK Saint – Scotland apart.) People had talked about shots of me looking glum as the rest of the England party celebrated as Hurstie put in that clincher in extra time. I can only say that if that were true then it was because I hadn't doubled my press bets. I will always regret missing out on a day that might never be repeated. It's not every day an Englishman gets the chance to hold that coveted trophy aloft. But I'll never forget the cheers and the waves of pride and emotion that swept over Wembley, and indeed the whole country, when my old mate Bobby Moore thrust the Jules Rimet Trophy skywards. I had missed out but England hadn't – and that was the main thing.

Alf Ramsey was the hero of the hour, and rightly so. He had moulded the England team into a skilled and efficient unit and gained his award. Shortly after the victory he was made a Knight of the Realm – and I couldn't have been more pleased. People often ask me what Alf Ramsey was like. To me he was the ideal manager. He cared about his players, had played the game at high level himself and had faith in a system which came under criticism but to my mind gave England her most successful team ever.

To most Alf appeared a cold, unapproachable man. But I'll bet that all those who played under him didn't find him like that. He was a Dagenham lad who bettered himself to be a first class full back with Spurs and England; he actually took elocution lessons to rid himself of his broad cockney accent. Even so Alf, now and again, let his 'H's' slip and I remember one particular pre-match England meal where he had us all doubled with laughter when the accent slipped as he told a waiter: 'Hi don't want no peas'. Alf was also fond of a gin and tonic.

This reminds me of one famous occasion during the 1966 World Cup period when the England party was invited to Elstree Studios for the making of one of the early James Bond films.

● *Norman Wisdom insists on giving me some practical hints on heading a ball...*

Alf, who recognised the need for highly trained athletes to be given a little rope, summoned us, told us to enjoy ourselves at the reception, but to behave! We certainly did enjoy ourselves. The wine and lager flowed like water and so, I suspect, did the gin and tonics!

At the end of a marvellous day during which we had been introduced to Yul Brunner and Sean Connery, Alf stood up to say a few words of thanks. In typical clenched-teeth Ramsey manner Alf said: 'Hi would just like thank h'everyone for a most memorable day. Your hospitality has been wonderful and I'm sure most appreciated by us h'all. And what a pleasure for us all to have met your stars, Mr.

Yul Brunner and Mr. SEEN Connery!' As the place erupted at Alf's faux-pas Bobby Moore, quick as a flash, chipped in: 'Gordon Bennett – I've SEAN everything now!' A few months later and Alf Ramsey from Dagenham was to become Sir Alf and, despite all those rumours, no-one was more delighted then me – except, I suspect, Alf himself!

MEXICO – FIRST TIME AROUND

Football, though, is a funny and a fickle game. Four years later England, as World Cup holders, might have beaten the odds and retained the trophy in the broiling heat of Mexico. That they didn't I believe was down to two things – Gordon Banks' illness at a vital stage in the tournament and the one major blunder Sir Alf made as England manager. This was the substitution of Bobby Charlton in the infamous match against West Germany in the quarter-finals when a 2–0 lead turned into a crucifying 3–2 deficit.

Gordon Banks is one of the most honest men in football and his views on being struck down with a gastric complaint just before the quarter-final tie against West Germany have always interested me. Banks was recognised in 1970 as the best goalkeeper in the World Cup and his importance to England was never more underlined than when making his much-talked about and shown save from Pele in an earlier round (Brazil won 1–0). He was surely destined to play a major part in the match against Uwe Seeler and company in Leon. However two days before the match he went down with suspected food poisoning. Later Banks, so weak that he couldn't even attend the match, reckoned he might well have been poisoned deliberately! His reasoning stems from the fact that he ate and drank exactly the same as the rest of the England squad yet only he was violently ill. At any rate Gordon could only look on from a sick bed as television showed up the lack of match practice of his deputy Peter Bonetti and West Germany snatched victory from the jaws of defeat – Bonetti being blamed for the final two goals from Beckenbauer and Muller respectively.

Peter was, and is, an old pal of mine but I feel he could be blamed only for the Beckenbauer goal

which put Germany back into the match. But the press needed a scapegoat – and chose Peter. Had Banks not gone down sick, either by accident or design, then England would have won that match and I believe would have gone on for another tilt at Brazil in the Final.

Strangely it was another incident from that game that, to me, signalled the beginning of the end of Sir Alf Ramsey's reign as England manager. Alf, of course, went on to qualifying rounds for the 1974 World Cup as England boss, only to be hounded out of a job when Poland pipped us for a place in West Germany. But it was his substitution of Bobby Charlton in Leon that was a blot on his distinguished career.

No game is finished until the final whistle but against West Germany in Leon Alf Ramsey pulled Bobby off when England were 2–0 up in order to save the player's 32-year-old legs for a semi-final match which never happened. I remember watching the game and saying: 'My goodness, what is he doing?' Charlton, as usual, had contributed much and even his continued appearance on the field would have worried the Germans. As it was Ramsey made the fateful decision to replace Charlton with Colin Bell and the rest is history. I've often felt that the 1970 England squad was superior to ours in 1966. Had England got through in Leon they would, I believe, have done what no European team has ever done before, namely have won the World Cup on the 'wrong' side of the Atlantic.

It was a tragic day, for not only did England go out but it was to be the last time that Bobby Charlton ever wore an England jersey. It was his 106th cap.

So much for the football. By the time England had reached Mexico so had I. By that time of course I had no pretensions of playing for my country again but Mexico saw me wearing another white uniform – that of a rally driver in the World Cup Rally!

In all my varied experiences in football none will compare with those in what was at that time the longest – and toughest – rally ever. Some bright spark had the idea of marking the 1970 Finals in Mexico with a World Cup Rally and being a sucker for impossible dreams I somehow got roped in! Actually it was sprung upon me in what I call my 'Lager Period'!

On the whole, Mexico 1970 was not a happy time for my old England colleagues. There was the scandal of the Colombians blaming captain Bobby Moore for the theft of an expensive bracelet, the unlucky defeat by champions-to-be Brazil and the stunning reversal by West Germany when a semi-final place beckoned.

Most of the players will, I'm sure, want to forget the land of sombreros and tequila. But not me. For while my mates were tuning up for the Finals I was tuning up too, not myself I hasten to add, but a very special Ford rally car which was to give me the biggest kick of my sporting career.

I'm often asked for my favourite sporting memory. Folk expect me to say my debut for England, some special hat-trick for Chelsea or Spurs, two winning Cup Final appearances or being part of the great Tottenham team which gave Britain her first European trophy. The answer often disappoints – for it's finishing fifth in the 1970 Mexico World Cup Rally!

That I survived, with honours, 16,000 miles of rough roads on two continents was amazing. That I survived *at all* was nothing short of a miracle! The most exciting three weeks of my life started off where many of my adventures at that time started – in a boozer. To be exact in the White Horse at Brentwood. This is the very pub, incidentally, where eight years ago I had my last alcoholic drink.

It was obvious that I was never going to be in contention for a World Cup spot in 1970 and, when a few mates of mine from Ford, particularly their then PR man Jimmy Graham, slung a few pints down me one lunchtime they managed to convince me that it would be a great idea if I tried my hand at getting to Mexico by car. It seemed easy. I was to have one of the best drivers in the rally world alongside me, Tony Fall, and I was to be given a thorough training in the not-so-gentle art of rallying at the army-vehicle assault course at Bagshot, Surrey. Since I always enjoyed driving, still do in fact, I was happy to have a

go. I mean what was 16,000 miles to a man like myself who had handled the crash, bang, wallop terrors of London motoring with only one or two little bumps to show for it.

Actually I should have bottled out after the training at Bagshot. The man who taught me to skid round corners, handle bumps which could easily force a man's voice a few octaves higher and had me driving over gullies on which the Army tested their tanks was Roger Clark one of the all-time British greats. Roger put the fear of death in me. I wanted to pull out but stupid pride kept me going and, after a week or so under Roger, I was aware of some of the troubles ahead. I was even more aware a week later when we went on a special recce in Yugoslavia, using many of the rough roads and wooded paths which look so nice on telly but are sheer bloody hell when you're having a go on your own.

I don't know why I didn't pull out. Maybe it was the fact that I didn't want to let the Ford lads down after their training. More likely it was just pure bloody stupidity. Anyway one fine summer's day in London Sir Alf Ramsey, my old guvnor, sent 113 of us on our merry way from Wembley Stadium. I chirped at Sir Alf: 'See you in Mexico'. Alf, always a master of the understatement, just looked at me as if I was daft and murmured: 'Oh yes, we'll see'. In fact I did make it, but not before some fairly hair-raising moments.

It was great – all the way to Dover. Then when we reached Calais the race was on. I took the first shift, so to speak, and drove solid for a day, a night and a day all the way to Sofia, Bulgaria. No sleep, very little food and a million scares along the way.

We then moved into the primes, the roughest parts of the rally. That's when Greavsie became the navigator and Tony did what he was good at – getting us up to the checkpoints in time. Tony, a tough Yorkshireman from Bradford, was marvellous and after a week I was beginning to get the hang of things. However there was one rather nasty moment in Yugoslavia where my navigating had us in, shall we say, a bit of trouble. Actually, as I told Tony later, it wasn't really my fault. On our way to a

● *World Cup Rally, 1970. I don't know why I didn't pull out...*

checkpoint on some mountain in Yugoslavia a bridge had disappeared but I soon found another way through – by driving the wrong way up a railway track at two o'clock in the morning. I got us there, but I reckon Tony only realised that after he opened his eyes! At the end of the European stage of the Rally... 8,000 miles which had seen us slither and snake our way through Europe to Lisbon, we were in tenth place – not bad considering it was amateur's night out where I was concerned.

I was, of course, absolutely knackered. Every bone in my body, and every ounce of logic, told me

to give up – but again that old enemy pride kept me at it. It was a bit, I suppose, like being at war. You don't want to be there, but once there you make the best of it. I told myself, as the boat took the cars off to Rio, the bloody thing might sink and that would be the end of it all. In my heart of hearts I knew that wouldn't happen and a ten-day rest back in England helped refresh the old Greavsie batteries. Soon Tony and I were flying to Rio to re-commence battle.

That things were not going to be easy had been brought home to me very early on. We left the centre of Rio to the catchy rhythms of samba bands but only a mile further on we came across a dead body. Some poor soul had been killed in a road accident, exactly the thing one didn't want to see starting an 8,000 mile stint through some of the roughest driving terrain in the World. On the outskirts of Rio the tarmac road stopped dead and suddenly we were on the dusty dirt roads which were to become commonplace as we motored through Brazil, Uruguay and Paraguay. Each stage was 56 hours with only eight hours sleep in between. We moved on quite well and by the time we got through the pampas lands of Argentina I was doing the primes as well. I remember well the scenery of Argentina – it was some of the most spectacular I'd ever seen – the only problem was I saw a lot of it on foot!

On one prime one of our wheels gave out on us and, in trying to get it off, the wheel studs sheered. Tony decided the only thing to do was to send me on in front looking for help. The old feet weren't what they used to be, what with some unkindly nudges from the likes of 'Chopper' Harris and others so I flagged down a local bus. I'll never forget the look on the peasant passengers as I sat in my rally gear in the middle of fourteen crates of chickens and a few screeching geese. Eventually realising I was getting nowhere fast I got off the bus in the middle of nowhere. I remember sitting on a stone looking around me and thinking to myself: 'What are you doing here Greaves. You could be sat back in your local with a pint. You must be mad.'

But help was at hand. The British Army, like the Seventh Cavalry, suddenly appeared from nowhere and told me that Tony had got the wheel off, and another on, albeit without any wheel studs. I had never been so happy to see anyone as Tony limping towards me. I thought I was lost in the pampas!

We eventually made it to our checkpoint, in time, but on the hub cap of the damaged wheel. I was just happy to get to civilisation but my joy was short-lived. I was soon down in the dumps again when I found out that, had we travelled the last twenty miles of that particular prime trouble-free, then we would have led the rally. As it happened the wheel trouble knocked us back to fifteenth place and, from that

moment on, we were only in the rally to survive. But it was a strange thing. The constant sleepless nights, the dangers and narrow escapes, harden one up. Tony was an old hand at the game but I could find myself becoming more determined to make it to Mexico. I hadn't gone twelve thousand miles to give up. Mind you before we were to reach Mexico City there were a few more nightmares to go through.

I was gaining confidence all the time and doing more driving but the car was suffering. We had to replace all the struts and shock absorbers in Santiago before we headed into the Andes. And it was thousands of feet up after splashing our way through disused mine tunnels I gave Tony the fright of his life. I was driving one night when I took the wrong fork in the road. Suddenly we were speeding head first down a mountainside, scattering a few llamas on the way. Forunately the road I had missed had wound it's way around the mountainside and we finished back on it – on the other side a few thousand feet of gorge awaited us! That was a nightmare moment for both of us but the Andes made up for that the next night when they provided me with one of the most magical moments of my life.

We were 22,000 feet up a mountainside on a crystal clear night and as we stopped for a reviving cup of coffee the stars seemed almost within reach. The night was so still, the stars so bright, and the view below us so breathtaking we were both stunned into silence. The five minutes we spent on that mountain will live with me forever.

Another moment which I'll always remember also happened on a mountainside. This was in Peru when a band of armed rebels, complete with guns, stopped us and searched the car. They didn't cause any trouble; they were just curious. Some of them had hardly seen a car, let alone two strange blokes in rally uniforms in a souped up Ford Escort. After poking about for a few minutes they sent us on our way – and Greavsie breathed again.

If I was panic-stricken in Peru, I was petrified in Panama. It was there I almost had the RIP notices out. Tony had just taken over the driving and as we were trying desperately to make up time on the other drivers, I told him to get the boot down on 50 kilometres of a particular stretch of good tarmac road. I reckoned it was time to get a bit of shut-eye. Tony had the needle flickering at 100 miles per hour and had around ten minutes of motorway ahead. I had just closed my eyes when there was a colossal crash. I opened my eyes and the car was spinning in the middle of the road. Tony was working his arms like a windmill trying to gain control – and we were both covered in blood!

Tony, the expert, did somehow regain control but when we looked at one another and the state of the car we knew we had hit disaster. I found myself bailing out great lumps of flesh and blood which had filled the car. Was it human flesh and blood? Once we had recovered sufficiently we realised what had happened. We had hit a horse full on. But again we worried – was there someone on it? Thankfully the answer to that was 'no'. Our car, of course, was a mess. The windscreen had gone and the whole of the roof had been ripped off. We were lucky to be alive, luckier certainly than the poor horse.

Our next worry was whether the police were going to lock us up in some Panamanian jail. But when we told them our story they let us carry on. It was out of that lucky escape that came one of the funniest moments of the rally. As official Ford entrants we had the right to annexe any Ford parts to get us to the finish of the rally. And having just gone through hell we had no intention of giving up. So Tony drove us to the nearest village and went straight to the local Ford dealer. It was a real one horse town (and we had probably just killed the one horse!). In fact it turned out to be a 'one Ford' town. The only Escort in town was the pride and joy of the dealer. It stood proud and gleaming in his shop window – but not for long. For despite his protests Tony took it to bits to build our own car up again. Then off we went, laughing while the poor dealer tore his hair out at the roots. I've often wondered how long it took him to get a replacement.

The rally ended for Tony and I a few days later in Mexico City. We were welcomed at the finish by a typical Mexican band. We had finished fifth in one of the toughest rallies of all time and I'll never forget the glow of achievement which spread over me as we crossed the finishing line. I hadn't really wanted to do it but in the end it was worth it. I know now why rallying is such a disease with the men who take their lives in their hands on the world's worst terrain.

Those sixteen thousand miles, the spills, the thrills and the danger are indelibly printed on my mind today. Of course I have my football memories. But the Mexico World Cup Rally was my greatest sporting moment. And at the end of it all I even got to see Bobby Moore, much to the dismay of Her Majesty's Embassy staff in Mexico City.

As I said, the constant battle with the elements, rutted roads and the fear had toughened me up considerably. So when I arrived in Mexico to find that my old mate Bobby Moore was the compulsory guest of the British Embassy, because of the affair of the missing bracelet in Colombia, I was determined to see him – despite the fact no one, but no one, was allowed near him.

Most England fans will know the story well. Bobby, along with other England players, had visited a jewellery store in Colombia during a pre-World Cup tour. An expensive bracelet had gone astray according to the owner, and he blamed, ridiculously of course, Bobby Moore. It looked for a time as if England would have to do without their captain in the World Cup Finals. The Colombians seemed intent on keeping Bobby locked up until the case came to court, that was until the British Ambassador in Mexico got them to agree to let Bobby travel to Mexico City and 'lodge' at the British Embassy there.

Mooro, of course, was virtually under house arrest in the Embassy and when I arrived in Mexico City the whole of the British press seemed to be camped outside, with no hope, as they told me, of getting in. Having been through the rally mill in the previous few weeks little things such as protocol and security were not going to stop me consoling my old mate. So I took matters into my own hands – or should I say feet!

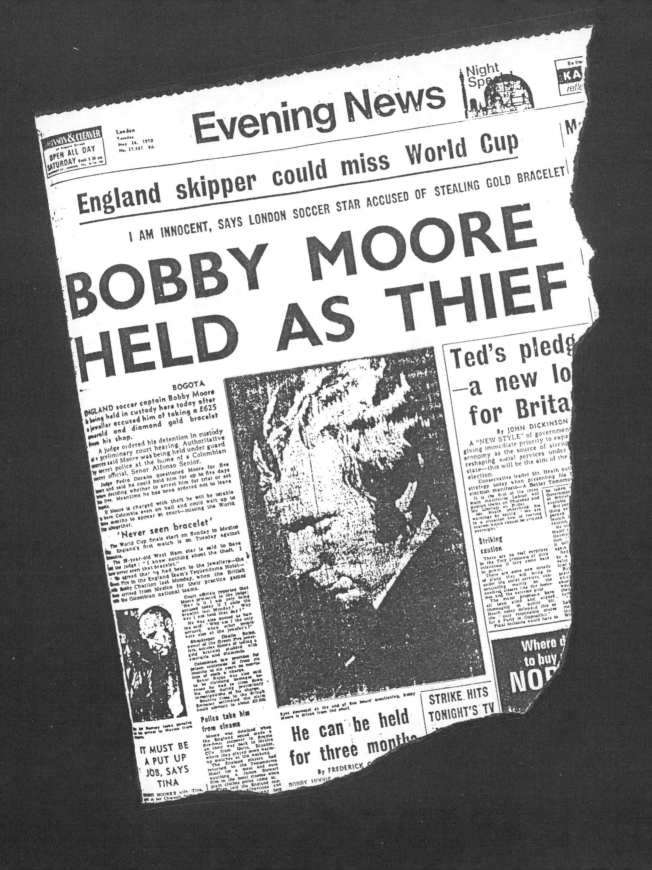

Evening News

London
Tuesday
May 26, 1970
No. 27,481 6d.

Night
Spe...

Be fr...
KA...
refle...

M-

England skipper could miss World Cup

England skipper could miss World Cup

I AM INNOCENT, SAYS LONDON SOCCER STAR ACCUSED OF STEALING GOLD BRACELET

BOBBY MOORE HELD AS THIEF

Ted's pledg
—a new lo
for Brita

By JOHN DICKINSON

A "NEW STYLE" of government
giving immediate priority to expa...
economy as the source of streng...
reshaping social services under
state—this will be the aim of the ...
election.

Conservative leader Mr. Heath out...
strategy today when presenting his ...
election manifesto—A Better Tomorro...
It is the first of the three ...
main manifestos. Labour will
publish theirs on Thursday and t...
the Liberals on Friday.
Mr. Heath underline...
warnings by saying: "We are ...
in a situation now of roaring ...
inflation which cannot be stopped
overnight."

Striking
caution

There are no real surprises ...
in the Tory proposals of their
intentions if they come back ...
to power.
There are some new details ...
of plans they will bring in ...
under the social services, con-
centrating mainly on ...
the homeless and the extreme poor...
The major proposals have ...
all been aired and ...
thoroughly discussed in public ...
Heath today defends this as ...
the only responsible course ...
for a Party in Opposition ...
Final decisions would have to ...

Where d...
to buy
NOR...

BOGOTA

ENGLAND soccer captain Bobby Moore
is being held in custody here today after
a jeweller accused him of taking a £625
emerald and diamond gold bracelet
from his shop.

A judge ordered his detention in custody
at a preliminary court hearing. Authoritative
sources said Moore was being held under guard
by secret police at the home of a Colombian
soccer official, Senor Alfonso Senior.

Judge Pedro Dorado questioned Moore for five
days and said he could hold him for up to five days
while deciding whether to arrest him for trial or set
him free. Meantime he has been ordered not to leave
Bogota.

If Moore is charged with theft he will be unable
to leave Colombia even on bail and could wait up to
three months to appear in court—missing the World
Cup altogether.

'Never seen bracelet'

The World Cup finals start on Sunday in Mexico
and England's first match is on Tuesday against
Romania.

The 29-year-old West Ham star is said to have
told the judge: "I know nothing about the theft. I
have never seen that bracelet."

He agreed that he had been to the jewellers—the
Green Fire in the England team's Tequendama Hotel—
with Bobby Charlton last Monday, when the British
teams arrived from Mexico for their practice games
with the Colombian national teams.

Court officials reported that
Moore protested to the judge:
"How is it I am only being
accused today if I stole the
bracelet last Monday? Why
was I not held that day?"
He was also quoted as having said: "Why am I the only
one accused when other people
were also at the jewellers?"

Shopkeeper is Danilo Rojas,
owner of the Green Fire jewellers, accuses Moore of taking a
gold bracelet studded with
emeralds and diamonds.

Colombian law provides for
prison sentences of from six
months to six years on convic-
tion of such a charge.

Senor Rojas was also said
to be claiming damages because he had to close down his
shop during the preliminary
investigations of his charge.

Bogota close to the British
Embassy estimated the claim
could amount to about £3,000.

Police take him
from cinema

Moore was detained when
the England squad made a
five-hour stopover in Bogota
on their way back to Mexico
City from Quito, Ecuador,
where they played more warm-
up matches at the weekend.

The England side had
returned to the Tequendama
Hotel for a meal. Bobby was
watching a James Stewart
film in the hotel cinema when
plain clothes police came in.
They told him the allegations and
took the England cap-
tain...

IT MUST BE
A PUT UP
JOB, SAYS
TINA

BOBBY MOORE'S wife, Tina,
pictured at her Chigwell home

Eyes downcast at the end of five hours' questioning, Bobby
Moore is driven from the court

He can be held
for three months

By FREDERICK ...

BOBBY MOORE

An Ramsey looks pensive
on his arrival in Mexico from

STRIKE HITS
TONIGHT'S TV

Calmly going where no other Englishman had gone before I scampered around the back of the Embassy, scaled a twenty foot wall, dropped gently onto the back lawns, walked coolly through the kitchens saluting the startled chefs with a 'buenos dias senores' and marched straight into an ante-room where Bobby was sitting looking very sorry for himself. Bobby was the coolest player I've ever seen on a football field but he almost fell off his chair when I chirped: 'How're you doing mate?' Since the place was guarded like Fort Knox he was somewhat amazed to see me – but we had a good chinwag about his situation until an Embassy official walked in and almost collapsed as he spotted me.

Being a polite bloke, I introduced myself but was promptly whisked from the room. I stood by my rights. That rally had really toughened me. So, after a confab, they asked me to go out of the front door and then ring the bell. I did so, watched from outside the front gates by an astonished world press, and then they allowed me in to see Bobby again. Trust the British. They couldn't take the fact that I had got in through the back door and had to make sure I came in through the right entrance. After their early anger the Embassy staff were quite nice to me really. They made me a pot of tea, I had my chat with Bobby and I think it cheered him up no end.

Bobby was eventually cleared of taking the bracelet, and the fact that he went on to captain his country in the World Cup Finals in his usual, impeccable manner, with the threat of arrest hanging over him, speaks volumes for his character. He was hounded throughout the Finals by the world's press yet never once did that ice cool reserve, which made him an England great, crack. A lesser man than Moore would have been unable to take the abuse, harassment and scandal which followed him in Mexico. Yet he still went on to have a good World Cup. If only England had half a dozen like him today!

6 SCOTLAND, THE WORLD CUP AND IAN ST JOHN

As Greavsie loves to remind everyone I actually never made it to the World Cup Finals as a player – despite being part of what is generally recognised as one of Scotland's best ever international teams. And although Jimmy's experience in Chile seems to suggest that the 1962 World Cup Finals in that country were to be avoided, it is still one of my biggest regrets that I never reached them as a player. For Scotland it was a case of so near and yet so far – what might have been.

The Scotland side at the time was a good one. With players such as Dave Mackay, Denis Law, Willie Henderson, Davie Wilson, Billy McNeill, Pat Crerand, Jim Baxter, Alex Hamilton, Eric Caldow, Bill Brown, John White and myself involved we were capable, on our day, of beating any country. Indeed during one summer tour we slaughtered Spain 6–2 before their own fans. This was no easy task in the halcyon days when Real Madrid ruled European football.

That we didn't get to Chile was down, I feel, to injuries to key players such as Bill Brown, Denis Law and the Rangers wingers Henderson and Wilson. We had only one big opponent in our qualifying section – Czechoslovakia – who at that time could boast players such as Masopust and Popluhar in their midst. We lost in Prague and then beat them in Glasgow. Since, at the time, goal difference didn't come into the final tally both teams were ordered to play a deciding game in Brussels, and only in later years did it sink in how close we came to perhaps causing a real sensation in Chile.

The World Cup in 1962 was nothing like the event it is today. There was no worldwide television. No idolised superstars such as Pele, Cruyff, Beckenbauer, Platini or Maradona. There were great players around, of course, but since the lack of televised soccer did not take their superb skills into every home they were not appreciated as they are today.

Still we realised it was a major occasion when we stepped onto the muddy surface of the Heysel Stadium to play the Czechs. Despite atrocious conditions we played well against them especially considering we were not at full strength because of the aforementioned injuries.

We went into a 2–0 lead and I got them both. We actually led the Czechs 2–1 with nine minutes to go before they equalised and then went on to beat us 4–2 in extra time. Naturally we were disappointed but it was months later the importance of the defeat really got to us all. For Czechoslovakia actually made the World Cup Final, only losing 4–2 to the Brazil team that Jimmy and I feel were the best ever.

Of one thing I'm certain, players such as Dave Mackay, Denis Law, John White, Willie Henderson and Jim Baxter would have graced the World stage. A pity that in the end only Denis actually played in the World Cup Finals, an appearance in the twilight of his career in West Germany in 1974. Still, if I didn't make the World Cup Finals as a player, there is no doubt that successive World Cups have had a big effect in my future career as a broadcaster. And there have been some laughs along the way too.

If 1966 is etched in every Englishman's memory then it is in mine too, for an entirely different reason – it was the occasion I got a right roasting from the wife! I had gone to Wembley with Ron Yeats and

Billy Stevenson and with a minute to go, a train to catch and England leading 2–1, we were making our way to the exits when a roar told us that West Germany had equalised. Big Ronnie and Billy decided to catch the train but I couldn't be dragged away and I stayed on to watch England go on to clinch victory. It was a tremendous occasion and, as Bobby Moore and the lads paraded the trophy around Wembley, it was obvious that London was going to have a night of nights. And so it proved.

After the match – the 5.30 to Lime Street having long gone – I met up with old friends, the comedy writer Johnny Speight, Jim Baxter and a bundle of footballers; they were all excited over the victory and ready to celebrate. And celebrate we did. Speight took us all back to his home and held a massive celebration party – livened up by the arrival of Jimmy Tarbuck who, at that time, was appearing at the London Palladium. It went on into the early hours of Sunday morning at which time, of course, my buddies Yeats and Stevenson were safely tucked up in bed in Liverpool like good little boys – their respective wives having casually mentioned what good lads they were to my missus.

I arrived home late on the Sunday, mindful of the Rabbie Burn's description of a wife awaiting a wayward husband 'nursing her wrath to keep it warm'. Betsy was very good about it. 'Where the Hell have you been?' she stormed. 'There was extra time' I answered. Tarbie would have been proud of me!

One last point on the England World Cup win in 1966. Forget about the controversial goal awarded when the ball did not appear to cross the line. Forget too that it happened at Wembley. England beat good teams to get to the Final and they deserved their victory in it. They were worthy champions all right. And truth be told, Bobby Moore might still go down in soccer history as the *only* Brit ever to hold the World Cup Trophy aloft.

I didn't begrudge Alf Ramsey his success then, but I did have reason to dislike England's soccer knight some four years on. For then it looked as if he had cost me a golden opportunity to become one of the country's top football commentators. It all happened

● *The Scotland team which played against England in 1962. Back row (left to right): Hamilton, Caldow, Brown, Crerand, McNeill, Baxter. Front row (left to right): Scott, White, St John, Law, Wilson*

• *'World Cup Grandstand', 1970. Back row (left to right): Ray Wilson, Johnny Haynes, Ian St John, Noel Cantwell, Brian Clough. Front row (left to right): Wally Barnes, Bob Wilson, Jim Finney, David Vine*

when the BBC had a brainwave before the 1970 World Cup Finals in Mexico. They decided to try to unearth a commentator from the untried British public. It was a great idea and, in fact, there were over ten thousand entries. People from all walks of life who loved football and fancied themselves as a Brian Moore or Kenneth Wolstenholme entered and, under some protest, I was one of them.

I was still playing at the time but, because of my Liverpool connection, Radio Merseyside's sports reporter Gerry Harrison – himself now an ITV World Cup commentator and sports expert with Anglia Television – coaxed me into entering along with himself. I had some experience in radio alongside Gerry in a weekly sports programme on Merseyside, but I hadn't had a go at commentaries before. But after a voice test in Manchester the competition was really on.

I remember bumping into former Scottish international winger Graham Leggat in London when we were summoned there. There were others such as Tony Gubba, now a BBC sports reporter and disc jockey Ed Stewart all involved – a collection of football nuts looking for a place in broadcasting. The whole thing was great fun. There were a succession of dummy commentaries with contest-

Robling. We had tied, and Sir Alf, that well-known Scots hater, who had the casting vote, plumped for Idwyl. At the time I could have murdered him but, in fact, he did both of us a good turn. Idwyl, I understand, now works for BBC Wales in Cardiff and of course the 'final' appearance helped launch me into a new career. Strange though that Greavsie and I eventually got together – we both got the Ramsey axe in a final!

Idwyl did get part of a commentary to do in Mexico but after all the ballyhoo the BBC never did take him on as a network commentator. But Idwyl's lack of fame may have its advantages. Brian Moore, the well known ITV presenter, received a postcard addressed: 'Brian Moore, England'. A chuffed Brian was very impressed – he turned the card over, only to read: 'Piss off Moore'!

My own experience certainly taught me to appreciate the impact of television. To this day people still come up and talk of that competition. The BBC thankfully decided that I had shown enough to include me in their World Cup panel for 1970 – and what a hoot that was. There was a cast of thousands – Johnny Haynes, Noel Cantwell, Bob Wilson, Brian Clough, Ray Wilson and old Joe Mercer.

Joe, incidentally, gave me one of my biggest laughs in television in a World Cup. Like Greavsie I rate old Joe as one of my favourite people in football, and his knowledge of the game is legend. But in those early days of panels he was inclined at times to mix up his names. On one occasion, while watching the great Holland team of the seventies, he came up with a classic when he said: 'I think that number fourteen for Holland is a marvellous player... that Johan Strauss.' Music to viewers' ears!

Getting back to the 1970 panel – that was my first introduction to the stormy, and at times contro-versial, ways of Brian Clough. In later years I was to join Cloughie on ITV World Cup panels and get to know his single-minded opinions on matches and players. (Who will ever forget him branding Poland goalkeeper Jan Tomaszewski 'a clown' after he

ants speaking over pictures of old matches. I read scripts, made up thankfully by Gerry Harrison, who, incidentally, kept getting through the various rounds in tandem with myself. Eventually though it all came down to a live TV programme where a panel of judges, which included Sir Alf Ramsey, had to adjudicate on the six finalists.

We all sat behind screens as our various commentaries were heard. We were only silhouette figures to the judges who voted on our football knowledge, voice etc. It was a bit like the Eurovision Song Contest without Terry Wogan. As each judge voted, the points registered against our shadows, and I realised I was in the running. In the end it was a straight choice between myself and a lad called Idwyl single-handedly stopped England qualifying for the 1974 World Cup Finals in West Germany.) But he excelled himself in 1970. Bob Wilson, as most readers know runs BBC's *Football Focus*, the opposition programme to *Saint and Greavsie* on a Saturday afternoon. But in 1970 Bob, like the rest of us, was new to the game and he inadvertently suffered the wrath of Cloughie in an amazing incident.

England were playing on this particular evening and I believe had been beaten by Brazil. Frank Bough, who was hosting the panel, at the end of the match turned to Bob Wilson and asked: 'How do you think Alf Ramsey feels... and what can he do now?' An innocent enough question and one which Bob answered to the best of his ability. But Clough turned apopleptic after the show. He castigated poor Frank Bough at having asked Bob Wilson – a goalkeeper – the vital question rather than himself as a manager. The BBC and the rest of the panel could hardly believe it when he raged on and then finally packed his bags and set off home saying 'I'll not be back'. It took the BBC days of coaxing and cajoling to get Cloughie back – but he did eventually return.

Like Jimmy I remember the 1970 World Cup Finals for the collapse of England against West Germany in that infamous 3–2 match after Ramsey's men were leading 2–0. It must have been a shattering experience and I remember at the time hearing that Alan Ball was so disappointed that he threw his tournament medal out of his bedroom window in frustration. I can understand that.

I don't agree with Greavsie though that England would have won the World Cup again – Mexico belonged to Brazil. Rivellino and company would never have been beaten in the end.

Another medal story from those finals is a touching one. Tostao the marvellous little Brazilian striker, who had serious eye problems, gave his winner's medal to the American surgeon who, a year earlier, had performed a delicate operation which allowed him to play again. A special story, since not many people have that winner's medal in their collection.

● A Rest of the World XI, Back row (left to right): Zico, Johan Cruyff, Karl Heinz Rumenigge, Diego Maradona, Paulo Rossi, Socrates. Front row (left to right): Harald Schumacher, Marco Tardelli, Jean Tigana, Michel Platini, Franz Beckenbauer.

I finally made the World Cup Finals in person in 1974 – as a football manager! I was, at the time, manager of my first senior club Motherwell and went to West Germany to learn from the greats along with a posse of other managers. It was valuable experience but I can't help feeling sorry even now for those marvellous Dutchmen, Cruyff, Neeskens, Krol and company who to my mind were the best team since 1970 never to win the World Cup.

Their final appearance in 1974 against hosts West Germany is now soccer history. From the opening whistle they made fifteen straight passes without a German touching the ball before Johan Cruyff was brought· down by Uli Hoeness and the English referee gave a penalty which Johan Neeskens converted. Later in the game Taylor awarded the Germans a penalty which even now looks a dubious decision. West Germany went on to win in extra time – but don't tell me they deserved it.

As a Scot I must also point out that my own country were most unlucky not to progress beyond the first round in 1974. The Scots beat Zaire 2–0, drew 0–0 with pre-Tournament favourites Brazil and then drew again, this time 1–1 with Yugoslavia. I remember well the night of the goal-less draw with Brazil. Davie Hay, the quiet destroyer hit the crossbar with one shot and then Billy Bremner was inches away from notching the goal our second half performance deserved.

As I've mentioned, many critics felt that the Scotland team I was priviledged to play in was our best since the war. The 1974 squad which consisted of players such as Bremner, Law, Jimmy Johnstone, Jim Holton, David Harvey, Peter Lorimer, and the exceptional young talent of Kenny Dalglish, Danny McGrain and Joe Jordan alongside the resolute Hay was also exceptional. It's worth remembering that it had got off the worst possible pre-World Cup start – with the infamous Jimmy Johnstone rowboat story at Largs.

For those who have forgotten I can tell it in the late Willie Ormond's own words. He was, at the time, Scotland manager. Willie, a gem of a man, once told me how he discovered the Johnstone

incident which had non-Scots hooting with laughter and my fellow Jocks burning with anger. It occurred on a warm May night before the international championship decider with deadly rivals England at Hampden. The Scots had lost surprisingly, to Northern Ireland but then retrieved themselves by beating Wales at Hampden – I let Willie take up the story:

'It had been a good night against the Welsh and it turned out that England had been beaten by Northern Ireland... a Terry Neill goal at Wembley giving the Irish their first win over England since the War. So I gave the lads a night off. Largs isn't one of the fleshpots of the World you know and all they could do was have a good drink. I had had one or two myself to celebrate and got to my bed around midnight and fell into a deep sleep. Around five in the morning I was awakened by the chants of "Scotland, Scotland" and thought to myself "what the hell are those fans doing here at this time of the morning?"

'Our hotel was on the front at Largs and eventually, as the sun streamed in my window, I was aware of a bit of a commotion on the seafront... so I got out of bed to take a look. I almost fell out of my window... for there about a couple of hundred yards from the shore, bobbing about in a rowboat, waving one oar was little Jimmy Johnstone. It was he who was chanting "Scotland, Scotland" and the rest of the squad were in stitches on the front. I thought! "Hell – if this ever gets into the press we're all sunk" and made a bee-line for the door still dressed in my pyjamas. But as I reached the front door of the hotel a coastguard cutter came hoving round the bay to rescue wee Jimmy and, as the fishermen gathered on the front, I knew there was going to be a major scandal in the national press.'

And Willie was right. The national press had a field day. The Scots were enraged that such an incident should happen before a Scotland–England match for the international championship. The rest of the World treated it like a gigantic joke – particularly with the Scots being Britain's only representatives in the World Cup Finals in West

Germany.

But strangely enough the few days of criticism sparked that determination which can set the Scots apart from others. On the Saturday, given little chance of success they went out to beat England at Hampden and win the international championship – just the boost they needed for the Finals. And Willie Ormond also used to look back on one related little incident which he felt got the lads laughing just in time for the clash with the Auld Enemy. As the Scotland coach was rounding the front at Largs Jimmy Johnstone was sitting in the front seat.

A typical Scots punter was passing – bunnet and muffler still on despite the scorching weather – and he caught sight of wee Jimmy and gave a great imitation of a goldfish, moving his arms in a breaststroke action. Ormond told me: 'The whole bus erupted with laughter. The crisis of the past few days was over and we were in the right mood for England.' And so it proved later for the World Cup Finals too.

I enjoyed my trip to West Germany for the 1974 Finals but have to admit that it had nothing on my next view of the World Cup Finals – from close range in Argentina in 1978. Needless to say it was a disastrous trip for the Scots. Beaten by Peru, held by Iran before beating eventual finalists Holland in our last first stage match. There was the Willie Johnston drugs drama and there was Ally MacLeod. Poor Ally. He was crucified by the media for telling the Scots what they wanted to hear – that their team was good enough to come home with a medal.

I repeat: he said we 'could' win a medal – not that we 'would' win the World Cup like Ramsey declared in 1966. Certainly on paper it looked as if the Scots had a good squad, with players such as Don Masson, Bruce Rioch, Graeme Souness joining Dalglish, Archie Gemmill, Jordan and Johnston in South America.

But the rest is history. Scotland got off to a good start with a Joe Jordan goal against Peru but then Don Masson missed a penalty at a vital stage and the evergreen Cubillas rifled in two free-kicks to eventually give Peru a 3–1 victory.

Soon after this Willie Johnston was found to have taken a banned pill. I'm sure it was stupidity which made Johnston take the pill. After all it was a stimulant and fleet-footed Johnston was the last player ever to need any extra stimulus. Nevertheless the whole incident was unsavoury and the Scottish F.A. rightly sent Johnston packing – back home to Scotland.

In the end the whole thing was a shambles with Ally MacLeod the obvious scapegoat. Ally was a broken, miserable figure as he hosted his very last press conference. Castigated by the Scots and held to ridicule by the rest of the world he was a sorry looking figure as he turned to the waiting press and looking at a mongrel dog sniffing around his legs said: 'Here I am, not a friend in the whole world except this mongrel dog.' He bent to pat the cur which then proceeded to bite his hand!

Actually it's not generally known but I was the only Scot to come back from Argentina with a medal – but even Ally MacLeod, I reckon, would not have wanted it under the circumstances. It happened when I was on duty for ITV in Mendoza. I was on my own keeping a watching brief on one of Scotland's opponents when I heard that there was a chance of a game of golf. Being a golf nut I duly got an invite to the local club who were hosting a big amateur jamboree. This included a special section for the World's media who, of course, were present en masse in Argentina for the World Cup. At the presentation later it came round to the winner of the Media Medal. I was pleasantly surprised when the master of ceremonies announced: 'The winner of the World Media section... Mr. Ian St John of ITV, Great Britain.' I hadn't had a great score but was delighted to collect the medal, and happy too for the round of applause I got. I had arrived in world golf!

It was only later, after a few drinks and feeling like Sandy Lyle, I asked my host: 'Just how many entered the World Media section?' There was an embarrassed silence before he answered 'one'. Even the drink didn't help!

One other funny moment from Argentina I'll always remember was the night before Scotland were due to play Holland in their last section match. As the press corps drowned their sorrows, in breezed England manager Ron Greenwood to the bar. Ron was, if I remember right, a FIFA observer at the World Cup Finals and his last match before departing Britain had been at Hampden where England had beaten the Scots 1–0 with a hotly disputed goal. 'What are you worried about lads?' joked Greenwood. 'All you need to do is beat Holland by three clear goals and you're through.'

Ron was treated to some withering looks from the Scots and that doyen of Scottish sportswriters Hugh Taylor, then of the *Daily Record*, retorted: 'What do you mean beat Holland ... hell man, we canny even beat you.' Exit a flushed, and slightly smaller-looking, Greenwood.

If Argentina was a disaster for my country, the 1978 World Cup did provide me with one of the great moments of my life – I played alongside my great hero Alfredo di Stefano. It all happened in Buenos Aires when someone had the bright idea of hosting a South American media team against a European media side. I was included in the European forward line which read Kopa, Fontaine, Di Stefano, Bobby Charlton and me. Quite a line up and when you consider we had backing us up players such as Facchetti, Jack Charlton and Billy Wright in defence we fancied ourselves a bit. That was until we looked at the other line up. It consisted of players such as the great Gerson of Brazil, Sivori of Uruguay and a host of other players who had been football heroes in their own South America and still looked fit enough to play.

The game was a cracker. Fifteen thousand fans turned up to watch us draw 5–5 and my one moment of glory came when, anticipating the famous Di Stefano one-two, I managed to put the maestro in the clear only for a swarthy Argentinian to come in and barge him off the ball. I would have died happy had he scored from my through ball. But, if I was happy Big Jack certainly wasn't – and that gave us all a real laugh.

The big fellow was feeling the pace a bit but, as usual, came loping up for every free-kick. The only problem was Kopa, the great little French player, wanted to take every kick himself. Three times he shot for goal – three times the ball ended up high over the crossbar. Jack, his long neck outstretched, then had to gallop back to his own half – cursing Kopa. He screamed at me: 'Tell that ****ing frog to wait until I get there.' Eventually another free kick was given on the edge of the South American penalty area. I managed to restrain Kopa until Jack arrived on the penalty spot – only for him to see his brother Bobby smash it high over! His reaction was unprintable.

7 GREAVSIE AND THE SCOTS

As anyone who watches *Saint & Greavsie* on a Saturday afternoon will know, the Scots in general, and Jock goalkeepers in particular, have taken a fair amount of stick from me. I've been called the 'Hammer of the Scots', an 'English Git', a 'Sassenach Loudmouth' – and these are just the nice things. Some of the contents of letters I've received from certain 'gentlemen' North of the border would curl the sporran on a Highlander's kilt.

But I'll let you into a secret – it's all a gag, and one that's lasted for over twenty years. It's true, I'll have a go at any daft goals or stupid mistakes we get from Scottish TV action. But the truth of the matter is that I'll have the same go at English mistakes. The Scots are more touchy than we Sassenachs, more aggressive and maybe that's why so many are such fine footballers. Every good Scots footballer has that little bit of devil in him which makes him stand out in a crowd – and no-one appreciates that more than me.

Many of my great mates in football such as Alan Gilzean, John White and Dave Mackay were Scots. And although I get my share of hate mail from Scotland most of the letters are complimentary. The true Scottish football fan knows I'm only getting my own back for the stick they all love to give the English. I'm often in Scotland on business these days and I never get anything but the warmest of welcomes. In fact one of the biggest thrills I've had during my television career is the welcome laid out by the Glasgow Lord Provost, Sir Michael Kelly – the man behind the great GLASGOW'S MILES BETTER campaign – and the reception at Celtic Park later from the Glasgow public. And all this is after some of the good-natured stick I'd dished out on the box to the Jocks.

So why do I have a go? Quite simply it was because I was fed up at the Scots having a go at the English without reply. When I joined up with Ian I told our producer, Bob Patience: 'I want to have a go back. I'm sick of your lot having a belt at us without getting one back.' As you've guessed Bob, like Ian, is a dyed-in-the-wool Scot but he gave me the all clear and things blossomed from there.

It's strange. At first the Scots didn't like me chirping back but then as they realised it was all in good humour they took it really well. Now I enjoy the walk to the big matches amongst them. Like the Cockneys and the Liverpudlians, the Glaswegians are very humorous and quick-witted.

I'll never forget walking to the Wales– Scotland World Cup tie in Cardiff this year. The streets were heaving with kilted Scots but there was never a bit of bother and I found myself laughing and joking with a group of them. One huge Glaswegian with tammie, scarf and outsize kilt hove to and shouted: 'Hey wee man... who do you fancy the night then?' I answered: 'Scotland... but I also fancy seeing what you've got under that kilt.' 'Nae bother wee man' he roared – and then proceeded to show me he was a true Scot!

As I say I think the Scots realise I'm being honest with my criticisms and appreciate that. They are certainly honest in their own appreciation of a footballer, whether he be English, Irish, Welsh, Brazilian or African – and that has always been the case.

Bobby Moore, my old mate, used to get special stick from the Scots when he was in his prime. 'Bobby Moore, Superstar . . . walks like a woman and wears a bra' they would taunt. But Mooro would always get a good reception after the match if socialising in Scotland. The Scots appreciated him as a great player. They might hate him for ninety minutes but they knew his value alright.

And the same with George Best. I remember Bestie telling me of the reception he got in a particular match at Hampden Park. They disliked the fact that Georgie might turn their team over but they applauded his talent – and that's what being a true fan is all about.

I suppose the Scottish goalkeepers gag goes back to while I was playing for Spurs. In those days only the BBC did preview programmes and of course, before matches, the whole team would crowd round the old black and white set to watch the action. And even the Scots used to shut their eyes when the Scottish action came up. The coverage itself was bad and so I have to say were some of the goalies and the defences. Actually we used to love the blunders but sometimes they were enough to make the iron man himself, Mackay, weep. It's strange too that, since I've teamed up with Ian, the goalkeeping mistakes have kept on coming. I remember praising Dundee United's Hamish McAlpine for an outstanding performance against Manchester United at Old Trafford and promising, as a New Year's resolution, never to criticise the Scots keeper again. On New Year's Day Hamish, playing against St Mirren I believe, made the worst blunder of his career. To be fair to Hamish it was freezing cold and he had had nothing to do until the final moments – hence the blunder. But bang went Greavsie's resolution!

It's true I do try to take the mickey out of the Scots but I only get away with it because they know I respect them both on and off the field. And I have had my moments – both good and bad – against Scotland on the field of play.

The Saint will never forgive me but I really have to mention England's biggest ever victory against Scotland at Wembley. It was 9–3 in 1960, a Flodden-like result which can still reduce hard men to tears in the bars around Sauchiehall Street. Actually I was involved in the goal which turned everything topsy-turvy for England – and I remember it as if it was yesterday.

We had been 3–0 up and coasting but the Scots, including Mr. St. John, were showing a lot of spirit, and had got us back to 3–2. We were really struggling to regain control. Then we were awarded a free-kick on the edge of the penalty-area. As the Scots were organising the wall I cheekily slipped the ball to Bryan Douglas and the little man went scurrying past the Scots defence and put the ball into the net. The Scots went mad. The referee had never blown his whistle and they reckoned they had been robbed. At the end of it all though we were 4–2 ahead and from that moment on we never looked back. In the end we scored nine and Frank Haffey, the Scots goalkeeper from Celtic, became a legend. Frank, who I'm told eventually went to Australia and became a nightclub singer, was crucified by the Scottish press who were out for a scapegoat.

The stick in the League dressing rooms at the time of Scotland versus England matches is always merciless no matter who wins. Since we had won on that occasion the patter went like this: 'What's the time lads?' 'Nine past Haffey' the reply was chorussed back by the English lads as the Scots in the team gritted their teeth in anger – that's if they had any!

I've often looked back on that famous match and sympathised with Frank Haffey a bit. He was crucified; nailed to the cross by press and fans alike, but to my mind he was to blame for only two of the goals. It's a strange failing of the Scots. They will defend their keepers to the hilt against my comments on any inadequacies but they are first to banish them if any team, particularly England, knock a few past them. Yet when we reached 4–2 in that game their defence was as wide open as a barn door. Banks, Clemence and Shilton together wouldn't have stood a chance with that defence in front of them.

Stewart Kennedy, the Rangers keeper, was another who got it in the neck when England beat

Scotland 5–1 in 1975 but yet again I think he was dealt with unfairly. I remember watching the game on television and while he was to blame for two of the goals the other three were down to poor defensive work by his team-mates. In the Scots back-four that day were giant figures such as Gordon McQueen and Frank Munro yet I well remember Kevin Keegan rising alone on the six-yard line to nod home unchallenged.

They say goalies are daft and I reckon they must be to take the stick they get. Strange how it's never the men in front of them who get the blame.

But if I enjoyed that 9–3 match I didn't enjoy the following year at Hampden, when the Scots got their own back for the cheeky free-kick they reckoned turned the match England's way at Wembley. The game will go down in Scottish football history as the first time they had beaten England at Hampden since the war. The final score looks convincing, 2–0 to the Jocks, but to this day I vow they had Dutch referee Leo Horn to thank for their win.

Again it was a controversial incident which turned the game. Again I was involved – but this time one of the worst decisions I've ever seen went against me. Scotland were leading 1–0 when I outstripped Eric Caldow on the right wing. I crossed quickly and there was Johnny Haynes to ram the ball at the underside of the Scottish cross-bar. I swear the ball was at least a foot over the line – a fact later verified by newspaper pictures – but somehow it spun back out and Billy McNeill smacked it over his own cross-bar for what was, at the very least, a corner-kick. Instead, amidst uproar in the English ranks referee Horn gave a goal-kick. We were raging but referees never change their mind and that was our last chance. The Scots went on to clinch things, ironically with an Eric Caldow penalty. Revenge must have been sweet for St John and company that day!

As I've mentioned I like the Scots. They are football mad and their support for their national team is to be envied by all. Wembley belongs to them every second year when those daffodil-yellow lion-rampants move in unison to the songs of the tartan hordes, swamping every English banner. Sometimes I think I'm the only Englishman there, apart from Brian Moore up in the commentary box.

Apart from the Scots as fans, some of the players are amongst the best I've ever seen. I've talked about Dave Mackay, the barrel-chested lionheart with whom I shared my glory days at Spurs. Dave, of course, was a Scotland regular yet I do feel he never quite reached his Tottenham standards with his country – and that was strange. Then there was Denis the Menace, the Lawman. He was my favourite player of all time. If George Best was the greatest player I've ever seen, then Denis Law was my idol. He was a typical Scot, jaunty, aggressive, fiercely competitive and like quick silver before goal. I suppose Denis was my counterpart in the Scotland team of the sixties.

Certainly I loved the man – and I know he felt the same about me. I've always had my bit of fun with the Scots but, although they tried, the press could never get me to say anything wrong about Denis. I have too much respect for the man. Throughout our careers the press would try and get us at it: 'They say Greavsie is better than you'. 'People reckon Denis is sharper in the box than you Jim.' They were waiting for that old England–Scotland rivalry and pride to ignite and get us both into a slanging match. But we were both too fly for them. Denis and I were mates. We competed on the field but no-one could split us off it. We had too much respect for each other for that to happen.

It's strange that Scotland didn't qualify for a World Cup in the sixties. They had a fine team in those days with Caldow, Mackay, McNeill, Baxter, Crerand, Henderson, St John, Law and Wilson.

I was pleased that Denis eventually made it to the World Cup Finals with Scotland in 1974 just at the end of his career. It was a fitting finale to a wonderful career and one that will never be forgotten. The Lawman was part of the Scotland side which every Scot claims rumbled England's World Cup winning side at Wembley in 1967 – 3–2 the final score in that one. The tartan faithful danced Highland Flings of delight after that win. I remember some fans cutting out little pieces of turf to take back on the overnight sleeper as mementoes of the day they brought the World Cup winners to their knees.

Actually it's true that they did beat us handsomely but in fact they did not beat the World Cup winning side – for I was in that team and not Geoff Hurst – something I believe to this day that old fox Ramsey, with his hatred of the Scots, planned in advance. It's fairly well documented that Geoff Hurst took my place in the 1966 World Cup side yet when it came to playing Scotland that day Alf put me in instead. I reckon he did that so that if England were defeated then the Scots could not claim they beat his World Cup team. Maybe he knew something we didn't before he sent us out that day. Certainly the Scots mesmerised us with some brilliant and skilful play – and no star shone brighter than Jim Baxter.

Jim, like myself, liked a jar or two and many people still slate him for putting himself out of the game far too young because of his boisterous lifestyle. Yet I claim that if you took that character, that devilment, out of players such as Baxter then they would not be the same on the field.

Certainly that day at Wembley belonged to Jim Baxter. He strolled his way through the match, his famous left foot flicking passes backwards sideways and forwards leaving many of my English colleagues stranded and red-faced yet unable to do a thing about their humiliation. Baxter enjoyed taking the mick out of the English, just as I do with the Scots, and I remember Alan Ball being left fuming as the bold Jim played 'keepy-uppy' with the ball tantalisingly out of range of the fiery mid-fielder. Baxter's display that day was the best I've ever seen from any player at Wembley – and I mean any player. If I hadn't been English I would have applauded him myself. It was a great performance by him and Scotland on the day but that old Scottish failing of wanting to show off and mickey-take rather than slam in more goals kept the scoreline to the narrowest of margins. And as I said, no matter what the Scots say – they didn't beat England's World Cup winning team that day. I should know, I was there!

One little Scot who never failed to entertain or amuse me was the great little right-winger of Glasgow Rangers, Willie Henderson. Wee Willie was an immensely skilful player in the mould of some of the Scottish greats of the past, players such as Alan Morton, Willie Waddell and Billy Liddell. He was an impish little bloke with a ready smile and he was as blind as a bat. I remember well the day at Wembley in 1963 when Eric Caldow broke his leg in a tackle with Bobby Smith. This was another day when Jim Baxter was Laird of Wembley scoring two goals, one from his first ever penalty, to beat us on our own ground. Jim might have been the darling of the Scots that day, but to me Willie Henderson was the greatest. The little man was quick, tantalisingly clever on the ball and his forays deep into our defence caused us all sorts of problems.

Willie spent most of his time in Scotland with Rangers, only moving down to Sheffield Wednesday at the end of his career. Had he moved when in his prime I'm sure he would have helped light up English football. Wee Willie also had a great sense of humour and one story which typifies him to me came from his own lips.

In his younger days, while still staying with his mother in Airdrie, he used to travel into Ibrox by train. In those days Glasgow Rangers, like Spurs, had a team of internationals. There were fine players such as Eric Caldow, Bobby Shearer, Jimmy Millar, Ralph Brand, Ian McMillan, Ronnie McKinnon and the peerless Baxter. Everyone, except perhaps the gentlemanly McMillan, was very capable of taking the mickey. Imagine, then, a teenage Henderson's panic at turning to a features page in the *Daily Express* as he was en-route by train to morning training and reading: 'We nominate the ten ugliest men in Scotland'. And there amongst the mugshots was Wee Willie himself!

Willie remembers his actions well: 'When I reached Glasgow city centre I decided to go and see my lawyer. I was raging as, thinking myself a bit of a lad about town, the newspaper feature was going to do nothing for my reputation. But as I was walking along St Vincent Street a teenage girl came up to me

and said: "Excuse me ... are you Willie Henderson?" Not being in any mood for nonsense I answered: "No" and walked on.

'About fifty yards on she came back again: "Excuse me, I think you are Willie Henderson." I turned on her saying: "Look, I've told you before, I'm not Willie Henderson, OK?" I was fuming but at least I thought I had got rid of her.

'Not a bit of it though. I walked another hundred yards and she was tugging at my arm. "Are you sure you're not Willie Henderson?" By this time I was getting pretty fed up. I turned and said: "Look ... I've told you twice already, I'M NOT WILLIE HENDERSON – NOW GET LOST." Whereupon she said: "Well I'll tell you something ... you're just as ****ing ugly!"' Exit the said lady leaving Wee Willie creasing himself on a Glasgow sidewalk!

That was Willie Henderson. A great winger on the field and a laugh-a-minute off it.

Looking back on the sixties I think how lucky Scotland was to have two wingers in quick succession, with Henderson first and then jinking Jimmy Johnstone of Celtic. Two marvellous players would be worth a fortune in today's inflated soccer market. Unfortunately there are not many players of that ability around today.

In recent years two Scots I've had a lot of time for are Graeme Souness and Kenny Dalglish. Souness has the leadership qualities I'm sure to go on and become a first class manager with Glasgow Rangers. His Hawklike attitude on the field has made him a dominant figure in British and international football. Ice cool, tough as teak, ever ready to create attack from defence. I believe that Liverpool were never quite the same when he left for Italy. They missed his natural air of command and his ability to slow things down.

Strange too that Graeme eventually wound up in Italy like myself. For I once gave him a bit of advice which, had Bill Nicholson known it at the time, would have sent him after my guts for garters. It was in the late sixties when my career with Spurs was coming to a close. Graeme at that time was a young apprentice at White Hart Lane and, even then, it was

obvious he had outstanding talent. But he was homesick for Scotland and one day he looked so miserable. I told him: 'Listen son ... nothing is worth being that miserable ... get yourself home ... leave here if you have to.' A few days later Graeme took me at my word. He walked out on Spurs in a blaze of publicity – and never came back.

Spurs had lost a player of exceptional talent and one worth a lot of money. The rest is soccer history. Graeme eventually signed for Middlesbrough, then for Liverpool and went on to captain them and Scotland. I still shudder to think what Bill Nicholson would have done if he'd known I had a hand in that one!

Kenny Dalglish, for so long the other cog in that Liverpool machine alongside Souness, and now Anfield player-manager, is another Scot whom I wish had had an English granny. To me Dalglish has everything. The aggression, skill, vision and shark-like finish before goal which makes a player great.

In the early seventies a friend took me to Parkhead to watch Celtic play an East European side. Celtic in fact lost the tie but I was greatly impressed by a blond youngster who, at the time, had just forced himself into the first team. It was Dalglish. The name stuck with me and I watched his progress. When he signed for Liverpool in 1977 for a £440,000 fee to replace Kevin Keegan I thought: 'What a bit of business'. To me it was probably the shrewdest buy of the last decade for there was no doubt in my mind that the Kop would quickly forget Keegan once they had Dalglish.

That wasn't me being clever. It's just that I believed then, and now, that Dalglish was a far superior player to Keegan. Little Kevin did well for himself. He was fast and strong but he had the lofty John Toshack to feed off at Liverpool. Dalglish had to forage on his own at times and still supplied the goods. Keegan twice won the European Footballer of the Year award. Good luck to him – but don't try and tell me he was a better footballer than Dalglish. King Kenny the Kop christened him and rightly so – now if Dalglish the manager can only unearth another like himself!

8 FUN FROM THE FANS

It's the fans that make the game – and much of the humour in it.
The Saint remembers:

s a Liverpool player I became used to the dodges certain members of the Kop would get up to just to follow the club all over Britain and beyond. One such Koppite was a fan who became known to us as 'Billy The Kitman'. Wherever we turned up he did. He watched every game and, to my knowledge, never paid for entry. His trick was to wait until the skip carrying the strips was unloaded from the coach and then take a handle – helping one of the trainers to carry it into the opposing ground. Once in that was it. He had gained entry and made himself at home on the empty terracings. As the ground filled up he became anonymous – except for the smile which said that he had diddled the authorities again.

The Kop, of course, is famous for its humour and on one famous night one wag put my old mate Jimmy Tarbuck in his place. It was Tommy Smith's testimonial night and Jimmy, a mad keen Liverpool fan, was allowed to don the red jersey and play. Jimmy was quite useful in his day, but, like the rest of us, the legs were not quite what they used to be. In one Liverpool attack he chased after a through-ball, never looking like catching it. As the ball sped further in front of the puffing Jim a voice from the terracing shouted: 'Come off Fattie... you're knackered!' Even Jimmy had to laugh at that one.

Trips with Scotland have provided me with many a laugh at fans' antics and in recent years during World Cups I've met some amazing characters. One such bloke is Big George Mulholland, a gravel-voiced Fred Flintstone lookalike who, despite living in Canada for almost twenty years, is still as broad Glasgow as the day he left. I say 'left' for George has got to go down in the *Guiness Book of Records* as the most travelled club football fan in the World. For George, a Glasgow Rangers fanatic, commutes from Toronto to Glasgow just to watch his team play.

George, a working-class bloke, has a simple game plan. He works on a construction site in Canada all winter, stopping only to sample some of the golden nectar his home country is famous for, and then, with what Arthur Daley would describe as a 'wedge', heads home for the closing stages of Cups, Leagues and Scottish internationals. Quite often Big George has been expected back in Canada at Easter after a three week stay in Scotland. Three months later I've bumped into him at the Cup Final or Wembley and he'll say: 'Never got back Ian... I mean the 'Gers are in the Final... how can you leave when they need you?' And he means it too!

Big George is also a great story-teller and, being part and parcel of the Rangers–Celtic scene in Glasgow, he is well versed in some of the hilarious gags attributed to the religious rivalry between the two clubs. For the uneducated, Rangers are the pro-Protestant club and Celtic the pro-Catholic. The bitterness which has evolved over the years is tempered at times with humour and one of Big George's tales is a gem.

The story goes that, at a time when Jock Stein's Celtic were winning everything in sight, the Rangers fans' morale was at a very low ebb. But one day, as they were queuing up outside Ibrox Park, this bloke turned up with a novel idea. He had a ball painted

with the Pope's face on it along with the message 'Kick The Pope – Ten Pence A Time'. The Rangers fans thought this great and soon the brainwave was earning the entrepreneur – let's call him Joe – a small fortune. The ritual went on for a few years and then one day Joe didn't turn up. In fact he never came back. Naturally the Ibrox fans missed their Saturday lunchtime fun and six months later one of them was walking down Sauchiehall Street when he noticed the aforementioned Joe. He approached him and asked: 'Hey, ... aren't you Joe, the bloke who used to stand outside Ibrox charging ten pence a go to kick the Pope?' 'Yes that was me' answered Joe. 'Then why did you give it up? The lads have really missed you on a Saturday.' 'Och' said Joe. 'I don't need to go anymore.. the Catholic Church is built noo!' That's Glasgow football humour – nobody escapes! One of the most hilarious tales in recent years also concerned a Scots fan, a club owner from Hamilton called Jim Tait.

When Scotland finally qualified for the World Cup Finals in Argentina in 1978 much thought was being put into how to get to such faraway shores by the kilted hordes. And Jim came up with a great idea – he would offer cut-rate terms to fans to go by submarine! Jim reckoned he could patch up an old German U-Boat, cram as many Scots fans in as possible, and make a nice few quid by transporting them across the sea to Buenos Aires.

It was all a gag of course but some press and even more fans took him seriously and he found himself inundated with offers. Jim's tartan submarine never reached Argentina but plenty of Scottish fans did. I was over there working for ITV in the World Cup and I met one fan who had hitch-hiked all the way from Glasgow. The Finals began in June and he had set off six months earlier, arriving just in time to see Scotland lose 3–1 to Peru in their opening match!

The Scots, of course, would follow the international team to hell and back – and in all modes of transport. For the World Cup Finals in Germany in 1974 they arrived in their hoardes in clapped-out vans and motor cycles, by coaches, trains and planes. And one abiding memory is of a beat-up Bedford van, full of Scots arriving at a particularly busy roundabout in Frankfurt. An immaculate German policeman was standing in his box directing traffic when a tartan-tammied head was thrust from a window demanding: 'Hey Adolf... what way is it to the Game?'

'Adolf' did not look pleased!

Of course, Greavsie can remember a few stories about the fans.

As someone who scored in my debut for my three top clubs Chelsea, Spurs and West Ham most of my memories of fans are good. I got off to a good start and that was the secret. But I did come up against some real London characters in my early days – football nuts who unconsciously did things that had us aching with laughter.

One typical punter was old Sam Harris, a Chelsea addict who used to manage the old Kilburn Empire Pictures House. Sam was a gem. He used to let all us young Chelsea lads in to see the latest movies and he would never miss a game at Stamford Bridge. But once, in the dark days of football before floodlights, we had an important mid-week match and Sam, desperate to see the game, told his Guvnor 'I'm ill... I can't manage in today.' The next day Sam was met by his boss who enquired sympathetically: 'Well Sam... feeling better are we?' Sam laid it on well: 'You know Guvnor. It must have been something I ate. I suffered something terrible. Dreadfully ill for 24 hours.' 'Yes' said the Boss. 'I could see you were suffering sitting in Row A Seat 23 at Stamford Bridge yesterday. You really looked in pain.' A startled Sam blurted: 'How the hell do you know?' 'That's easy... I was three rows behind you' countered his Gaffer. Game, set and match to the boss!

Those were the days in which, in London, if Spurs, Arsenal or Chelsea were playing in mid-week matches at least a hundred thousand grannies had died. I often wondered how the funeral undertakers coped!

Morris Keston, a long time Spurs fanatic, was another supporter who would do anything to see us

play. Morris, a great character, is Jewish and he paid the ultimate sacrifice to watch us play. We had a match in Egypt and, in those days of course, the Egyptians did not see eye-to-eye with the Jewish people. But so as not to be banned Morris took out a new passport and put his religion down as Church of England. Now that's what I call supporting your team!

Then there was old Johnny Goldstein – Johnny The Stick – who used to deal in tickets. And his minder 'One-armed' Lou. Johnny was a bit tasty and he used to have an interest in a club called Suki's which, I hasten to add, I never frequented but was well known to visiting teams. The Kray Twins were regular visitors and Johnny had a way of introducing star turns. The story is that he would introduce some budding singer saying: 'And here she is folks. The girl you've been waiting for... all the way from the Orient... LEYTON ORIENT!' Johnny was Stan Flashman's mentor. He taught Flashman all he knew about ticket spivving. Johnny could get you tickets for anything – including Buckingham Palace garden parties!

I remember my first day at Tottenham. Johnny The Stick sought me out and gave me the biggest rollicking of my life for daring to score for Chelsea against Spurs – a year earlier! He reckoned it had cost Spurs the championship.

I grew to be very fond of Johnny. Despite his trade he was a generous man and he helped many a Spurs player in the sixties and seventies. But he was so dedicated a Spurs fan that he gave me a roasting for having a pink cottage. 'With someone like you it should be white' he said. Johnny also had an intense hatred of Arsenal. So much so that he bought two season tickets for Highbury and, if we were away from home, he would go there and, from his seats right in front of the Gunner's director's box, he would barrack the Arsenal board for ninety minutes

and then go home happy. It didn't seem to occur to him that he was helping to finance his pet hate. Johnny might have been on the shady side of London life in business but he was an up-front guy with Spurs players. When he died every first team player went to his funeral. It was an all-ticket job and I'm sure he would have liked that.

London and Liverpool humour to me are very similar and two stories from the past still make me smile. The first happened when Chelsea built the new stand – the one that almost bankrupted them. It was a serious situation for the Stamford Bridge club but one fan had me laughing when he wrote to me after a particularly diabolical performance by the Blues complaining: 'Jimmy, there's been a cock-up in the design of the new stand... it's facing the wrong way.'

The Liverpool story naturally has a bit of red and blue in it for the great Liverpool–Everton rivalry never dies and Liverpudlians, being what they are, never lose a chance to score off the opposition. Now Tommy Smith has come in for a bit of stick over the years because of his hardness on the field – but I think this tale by the late, great Dixie Dean of Everton and England tops them all.

Dixie remained an Everton fan until his dying day... ironically in the Goodison stand... and when late in life he had a leg amputated he brightened up the rehabilitation clinic he was in by looking around him at a wardful of similar sufferers and saying: 'Come on now, who let Tommy Smith in here?'

In 1986 Bruce Grobbelaar also came in for a bit of stick from a home fan during a display which is best described as not one of Bruce's better days. Bruce had just lost his pet parrot in a burglary on his home but the unsympathetic wag cried: 'We were unlucky Brucie... he could have taken you and left the parrot!'

9 THE GAME IS FULL OF CHARACTERS

Football is full of characters – the cheeky chappies who boost team morale and can mean the difference between defeat and victory, agony and glory. Ian can recall quite a few of them.

Dave Mackay has already been talked about in other areas of this book as one of the all-time great footballers. He was also one of football's greatest characters and many a time during Scotland trips abroad he kept team morale sky-high with his pranks and patter. One memorable night was after a match against Turkey in Ankara, Mackay, as Jimmy mentioned earlier, was a bit of a punter and in a Scottish team which also included kindred spirits such as Bill Brown, Jim Baxter, Denis Law and Willie Henderson, Dave always was ready to do anything for a bet. But on that Turkish night he excelled himself – for he finished up dancing on the players' table before a horrified Scottish F.A. party and bemused Turkish officials.

It all started out as a gag. We had beaten the Turks 4–0 but our hosts, who must have been bitterly disappointed at the result, lived up to their reputation for hospitality and laid on a great after-match banquet. The local plonk flowed like water and Dave had his fair share along with the rest of us. In one corner of the room was a little three-piece Turkish band and it was the sight of them that sparked off Mackay. As the speeches droned on Dave, suitably fortified by the wine, was looking for a challenge, and he whispered to Bill Brown: 'Tell the lads I'll walk on the table if they all bet me a fiver.'

Bill put the proposition to us and, thinking Dave wouldn't dare, he collected around fifty quid. They say fools and their money are soon parted and since we knew Mackay's daring of old we should have known better. For no sooner had the money been collected than the bold Dave signalled the tinpot band to play some typical Turkish music and then mounted the table – making like Zorba The Greek! We, the players, were in stitches as the band, caught up in the action, played louder and louder. The faces of the officials got redder and redder and the Turks, surprised by the move, hand-clapped the Spurs skipper as he strutted along the table.

Some bright Scots official had a bright idea to avoid embarrassment. He told his Turkish hosts: 'An old Scottish custom... a way of thanking you for a marvellous banquet.'

By the end every player was choking with laughter, and the roar which went up when Dave eventually finished his spectacular was as big as was heard in the stadium that afternoon. Mackay had earned his fifty quid, but how he ever played for Scotland again after that escapade I'll never know!

One of the greatest characters I have ever had the privilege of working with was Bob Paisley, who was trainer of Liverpool under Shankly in the sixties. Bob, of course, went on to become the most successful manager ever in English soccer history, with seventeen major trophies during his five-year stint as Anfield boss. But he still has time to chuckle at the stories of the early days with Shanks. One story he tells in his Geordie accent is a real classic.

It was when we met Inter Milan in the European Cup in the sixties. We had won at Anfield and travelled to beautiful Lake Como to prepare for the second leg – and while the setting was spectacular Shanks wasn't happy. Bob told me: 'When you lot were in bed Bill suddenly realised that the church next door was ringing its bells on the hour, every hour. He told me: "Bob we've got to silence them... the boys must have their sleep."' Bob tried to put Shanks off but the boss was insistent and finally he and Bob arrived at the door of the church late at night.

Says Bob: 'Bill knocked on the door and eventually this monk came and opened it.'

"Liverpool Football Club" Shanks told the monk. "Here to play Inter Milan in the European Cup... your bells will keep our men from their sleep... could you stop them?"

'The monk was very pleasant about it all and explained to Bill. "Sorry ze bells cannot be stopped. Zese bells have rung this way for centuries. Is no possible to stop them just for ze football."'

'Bill of course refused to be put off and he pointed at me and said: "Then son do you have any objections if my trainer here goes up there and bandages them?"'

Bob told me: 'I was the most relieved man on earth when the monk said "No". I had visions of me doing my Hunchback of Notre Dame act up in the belfry, for knowing Bill he would have tried to muffle them!'

Another favourite Paisley story of mine also goes back to my playing days and of course the Shankly–Paisley double act again is involved. Shankly was a great man for innovations. We were always the first to have light-weight boots, super-slim shinguards, short-sleeved jerseys etc. So it was

no real surprise when he was off the mark quickly to bring the sensational German invention, the 'Black Box' to Anfield to treat our injuries. Until the introduction of the deep-heat system of the black box, injuries were treated in a rather haphazard way and many of the players of the sixties still limp around today – a legacy of bad treatment under the inexpert hands of amateur physios.

So when the black box arrived at Anfield, Bob was summoned along with the rest of us and the attendant press – Shanks was never one to miss a press trick – for the great unveiling ceremony. Bob duly unwrapped the black box and our first sight of Shanks' new toy was a tangle of wires, pads and dials. We needed a guinea pig and little Jimmy Melia, who later in life as a manager was to lead Brighton to an F.A. Cup Final against Manchester United, jumped on the treatment table and offered his injured knee for healing. Bob, hastened by an impatient Shankly, attached the pads to Melia's leg assuring the boss that he knew exactly what he was doing. The instructions were in German but Bob indignantly told Shanks: 'I know what it says... I was in Germany during the War.' Eventually Bob said 'That's it Jimmy... everything's fixed. Take this dial and just turn it. As soon as you feel anything stop.' Melia turned the dial but nothing happened. The titters were beginning – much to the annoyance of Shanks. 'Try again Jimmy' said Bob. 'Turn it on fuller.' Still nothing.

Melia turned the dial to full on. Yet again nothing, until Bob noticed that the plug in the wall hadn't been switched on. 'There you are man' said Bob as he bent down and flicked the switch on. Whereupon Jimmy Melia, still with the dial at full, almost hit the roof as the current surged through his leg. As the rest of us howled with laughter little Jimmy hopped around the treatment room screaming: 'I've been electrocuted! I've been electrocuted!' trailing dial, pads and Shanks' precious black box with him. That's one story old Bob doesn't tell too often!

But another story does highlight Bob's sense of fun. The manager had just completed the signing of Avi Cohen from Israel. A caller from Manchester

asked Bob if Avi was an orthodox Jew. 'Why do you want to know?' asked Bob. 'Well, if he is, he can't play football on a Saturday.' 'That's alright,' said Bob, 'I've got a few others like that already.'

It surprised many when Bob Paisley was so successful as Liverpool manager so late in life – but not me. Bob was always the buffer between Shankly and the players and his knowledge of teams and players was amazing. Often he would sit down with us and have ten minutes before a game talking football and his judgement was always spot on. The one thing that did amaze me was the way he handled the media. Bob was never one for the limelight. That he managed so well on and off the field only shows the quality of the man.

The new Liverpool manager, Kenny Dalglish, is known for his dry sense of humour. After the 1986 Cup Final he was asked by a newspaper reporter if he could explain why Jan Molby was playing so consistently. 'Yes,' said Kenny, 'he's playing better more often.'

Football humour in the city of Liverpool is not confined to Anfield – but at least most of Anfield's humour is intentional! One ex-Everton boss, Gordon Lee, has a history of clangers. His pre-match team talk before a derby match with Liverpool went as follows: 'Listen lads, Ray Clemence is not unbeatable. The fact that I think he is, doesn't mean to say that you should.'

Gordon Lee could never get to grips with foreign players' names. While sitting in a London hotel before a match he spotted Everton secretary Jim Greenwood and his wife.

'Why is Jim here?' remarked Gordon to his trainer. 'I believe he's down to see Evita' was the reply. 'Don't tell me he's down to speak to that little Argentine player from Spurs!' was Lee's reponse.

The current Everton boss, Howard Kendall, is a bit more thoughtful – but no less funny. Brian Clough and he had a difference of opinion after one Forest v. Everton match. Clough accused Kendall of being a 'young pup'. When asked to comment Howard replied: 'Sorry I can't say anything – I'm a hush puppy!'

Jimmy, who reckons The saint was daft to bet Dave Mackay anything, can remember great characters too.

Certainly a man I played with, and drank with, often had me double up with laughter at his antics. That was Johnny Byrne, the talented West Ham and England centre. Johnny was nicknamed 'Budgie' as he never stopped talking and, like Mackay, he was afraid of nothing. On one famous occasion though he went over the top. It's funny now but it was frightening at the time.

Johnny and I were in the England party which toured South America in 1964. I say 'toured' rather than played because it was a bit of a nightmare trip. We got cuffed 5–1 by Brazil, and were reduced to spectators in Sao Paulo as Brazil took on Argentina in a sort of mini World Cup Final. The problem was the tickets for the game were like gold and the entire England party had to watch from a bench on the touchline. The Brazilian fans caught sight of us and started singing 'Cinco-Una' which is Portuguese for 5–1. Sitting in the middle of 100,000 loony supporters all giving you vocal stick isn't exactly funny but Budgie couldn't resist the challenge. He jumped to his feet and began conducting the Brazilian choir – much to their amusement and pleasure. By the time Brazil and Argentina arrived on the field Budgie was the star attraction – then came the real fun.

The game between these two deadly rivals was a bloodbath with Pele getting it hot and hefty from an Argentinian thug named Messiano. Eventually the great Brazilian cracked. He turned and head-butted the Argie who was carried off with a broken nose. It was one of the clearest sending off offences I've ever seen but the referee, quite wisely I thought at the time, completely bottled it as the Brazilian fans shrieked like madmen. Pele was allowed to stay on the pitch but the mayhem knocked Brazil off their stride and the samba rhythms of the Brazilian fans were silenced when Argentina won 3–0.

It was at this moment Budgie Byrne delivered his coup de grace... and almost got us all lynched! He turned to his one-time Brazilian friends, now sullen at the thought of defeat from the great enemy and, holding up three fingers, invited them to join in a chorus of 'Three-nil, Three-nil'.

The crowd went wild. We were bombarded with stones, cushions, fruit and heaven knows what else. Even the ice cool Ramsey veneer was broken. As he copped an apple on his back, Alf got up from the bench and shouted: 'Right lads . . . leg it.' And leg it we did, straight for the centre-circle, uttering extremely naughty words at Budgie who by this time had realised his mistake. Mind you, give the old boy his due. It was he who realised that we still had to get down the tunnel without injury from the by now frenzied fans. 'Grab yourself a Brazilian' he shouted as he latched on the great Gylmar's arm. We duly followed suit and made it to the dressing rooms with the Brazilian fans deterred from their thoughts of murder by the close attendance of their heroes. It did teach Budgie and us all one lesson – even Brazilian fans only sing when they're winning!

Another character from back in the Bob Paisley era was the late, great John Cobbold. He was chairman of Ipswich Town and co-director, along with his brother Patrick, of the famous Tolly-Cobbold brewery. 'Mister John', as he was affectionately known throughout football, was one of my favourite people and some of the stories involving him are truly hilarious.

Once when asked by a reporter if he felt Ipswich were in a state of crisis his brother Patrick answered: 'Crisis? My dear boy what we consider a crisis here at Ipswich Town is when the boardroom has run out of white wine!' You can gather from that tale that the brothers Cobbold were fond of a tipple and Mister John occasionally got himself carried away while under the influence. My favourite story concerns the evening he laid on following the Ipswich Youth Team winning a major trophy. The brothers Cobbold, as hospitable as ever, provided a marvellous buffet, not only for the youngsters but their parents as well. As the night, and the drink, wore on Mister John gathered himself to make the obligatory speech.

'I would like to say how pleased we all are here at Ipswich at our Youth team's marvellous success. I thank the team, the manager and most of all you the parents. And what I would like all you good folk to do now is to have a good drink and go home and have a right good f***. Then we might be here celebrating another great trophy win in another sixteen years time!' A classic really, and football is the duller for the passing of John Cobbold who, once at the launching of a new sponsorship deal claimed: 'It has been suggested, most unfairly, that we will squander the sponsors money on wine, women and song. That is absolute nonsense. We don't do much singing at Ipswich.' People like Mister John are hard to replace.

Stan Mortensen, the great Blackpool and England centre-forward and still the only man to score a hat-trick in an F.A. Cup Final (1953), is a marvellous man and a great story-teller. He had me in stitches telling stories about his former manager Joe Smith, himself a famous goalscorer with Bolton Wanderers. Joe apparently had not only the knack of scoring goals but also of being an unconscious comedian. Typical of his verbal faux-pas was his description of the club spirit at Blackpool: 'We've got perfect harmonium in the dressing room' – and coaching a player: 'When you veer, lad, veer straight.'

Joe was a fine manager but Stan tells the story of how, before a vital relegation match against Cardiff away, when defeat would have sent Blackpool into the second division, Joe had his team in stitches. It seems he was never one for tactics or pep talks. He believed, like many good managers, in playing the game off the cuff. So when he ordered all the trainers and reserves out of the dressing room before the Cardiff match the eleven players, including the great Stan were deathly silent. It had to be serious. Could it be that Stan and co. were to experience a first – a Joe Smith team talk? Not a bit of it. Joe walked in grim-faced and said: 'I can't stress how important it is that when this game's over you get in and out of the bath as quick as possible.' Said Stan: 'We all wondered if trouble was expected. But we should have known better. Joe then hit us with the real reason. "We don't want to miss the 5.15 train back to

● *The Inimitable Pele*

● *'Well you see Ma'am, we all know each other.'*

Blackpool." Joe then walked out of the dressing room leaving us first dumbfounded, and then laughing. But it didn't do us any harm. We won the match 3–0 and caught the train.'

Finally a Danny Blanchflower story. You will have gathered from earlier chapters that I rated Danny very highly as player and motivator. He is also famous for his wit – something he had used to marvellous effect in his *Sunday Express* column over the years. And his humour was never more evident when, as Spurs skipper, he was presenting his side to the Duchess of Kent before the FA Cup Final of 1961. The Duchess asked Danny: 'Why is it the other team have their names on the back of their track-suits while your team do not?' 'Well you see Ma'am,' answered Danny, 'we all know each other.'

10 WHAT HAPPENED DOWN MEXICO WAY

MEXICO...SECOND TIME AROUND – Greavsie

The Mexican Mundial is over but the memories are still fresh in our minds. A billion people all over the world watched and heard (sometimes) the four yearly football fiesta unfold with the usual bubbling enthusiasm and excitement not to mention the Ola wave.

In the end Argentina were champions and Diego Maradona was the new King of World football. Good luck to them. The Argies were the best all round team in the tournament and the magic of Maradona was even strong enough to snuff the hex of me tipping them to win. (Take note St John... my second World Cup winners in successive tournaments.)

But I have a warning for the adventurous Argies, the dazzling Danes, the fabulous French, the brave Belgians and the scintillating Soviets... look out – England are after you!

For if Mexico '86 taught me anything as I sat goggle-eyed watching the box into the wee small hours, it was that England can win the World Cup again!

To be honest, for me the '86 World Cup was not one of the greatest. The Mexican fans' enthusiasm shone through the adversity which had beset them in the build-up and that was wonderful. And of course, we had marvellous moments when any one of eight teams looked capable of lifting Italy's crown. But in the end how many matches kept you rivetted to your seat in front of the telly until two in the morning? Not many if you really start to count.

Maradona, of course, will go down in history as the star of Mexico '86 and rightly so. Who will ever forget his fabulous goals against England and Belgium and his marvellous twisting, bull-like runs.

But my biggest kick from Mexico came from the growing knowledge that England can again win the World Cup. I have no doubt in my mind that the team Bobby Robson moulded there is capable of winning the European Championship in West Germany in 1988 and could even go on to lift the World Cup in Italy in 1990!

I don't say that lightly. For years English international football has been in the doldrums but suddenly it is all coming right and I'll go as far as to say that had the '86 finals been held in England, then Robson's men might have won them. I know my Jock friends will give me stick for saying it but the World Cup is once again no impossible dream for England, not with the squad that Robson has gathered around him.

People will point to the early group matches with Portugal and Morocco and claim that until such results are eradicated England can have little chance. I don't agree. England were in a no-win situation in that Group – it is always easier for a class team to be in against the best than minnows. From the Poland match on it was obvious that England at last had a team to be reckoned with. Under Bobby Robson they can only improve.

Let's be realistic. England were only a fingertip away (Diego Maradona's!) from at least holding the team who eventually turned out to be worthy champions. And I wouldn't mind betting that Peter Shilton, despite being one of the world's best, will have recurring nightmares about little Maradona beating him (albeit illegally) with that infamous leap in the Aztec Stadium. Had the Tunisian referee been as alert as the rest of the soccer World then England not Argentina might just have been lining up against West Germany once more in a World Cup Final.

If an England World Cup win sounds like pie in the sky, it's worth remembering that many of the players Bobby Robson selected for Mexico will also be available for Germany in 1988 and maybe even Italy in 1990: Shilton, still amongst the world's top three keepers; Terry Butcher, to my mind the best central defender in Mexico; Gary Lineker who won himself a golden boot and a place in the sun with Barcelona by finishing the tournament's top scorer with six goals; Peter Beardsley, the ideal foil for the ever alert Lineker; and, of course, Bryan Robson who with his shoulder pinned will, I'm certain, emerge over the next four years as a world class figure. Add to these, players such as Steve Hodge, Trevor Stevens and John Barnes, still only kids, plus one or two whose time has yet to come, such as Tony Cottee and Mick Harford, and Robson has a squad which I'm convinced will be a major force in the years leading up to Italy in 1990.

And a word about Bobby Robson. I rate him the best England manager yet. Of course Alf Ramsey was an astute man but Bobby brought a smile to the job despite the howls for his head at various times through the qualifying series and the group games. He kept his cool, took us to the last eight, and England left Mexico with dignity and respect. The FA should give him a chance until 1990. Bobby, an old international team-mate of mine, was a great ambassador for England in Mexico. He handled the pressures of a clamouring media well and was obviously passionately involved with team and country. His anguish for his team smashed through the world's TV sets following the defeat by Argentina. He's the man for the job alright.

Robson has done what neither Don Revie nor Ron Greenwood could manage. He's formed a sweet moving dangerous outfit which can put the fear of death into opposing sides.

One of my best memories of Mexico was the panic Argentina were in during the last twenty minutes of that quarter-final tie with England. Lineker was only inches away from an equaliser at one point and if that had gone in I wouldn't have fancied the Argies finishing up as champions.

I'm often asked my opinions of present day strikers and I must admit I'm not usually impressed. Take the World Cup for instance. It is a hobby horse of mine, but why must strikers blast the ball into the net from close range? I was a great believer in passing the ball into the net in my playing days and only Valdano of Argentina's goal in the final against West Germany stands out in my mind as a great striker's goal under pressure.

Not too many other strikers caught my eye. Laudrup and Elkjaer of Denmark were exceptions. Two great front runners with the skills to take men on and coolly slip the ball past a keeper. They are of the highest quality and Denmark are lucky to have them. Careca of Brazil was another. He was piranha-like before goal but strangely the Brazilians never quite gave him the service he needed. If they had done then they and not France might have progressed.

But the man who impressed me most of all in the six-yard area, which is the striker's domain, was our own Gary Lineker. For six years I have been singing his praises. I watched him a lot with Leicester City in my role as football expert with Central Television and the man oozed goals. He is sharp as a tack and it amazed me that it took a top English side so long to snap him up. Everton's £800,000 fee was well spent. Now a year later he is with Barcelona and his partnership with Mark Hughes will surely be one of the most exciting in Europe. Everton are left with £2 million profit in the bank... but will they win trophies without him?

Lineker has insisted that he be released for England matches by Barcelona and that is good news for Bobby Robson. Now that he has established a relationship with that great little Geordie Peter Beardsley, England could have a partnership to fear for years. My fellow World Cup panellist Kevin Keegan, who played with Beardsley at Newcastle United, rated Beardsley 'the best in

England' during the World Cup. Certainly he has taken over Keegan's mantle as a St James's Park folk hero and he took his chance well in Mexico. How another ITV man Ron Atkinson must regret him being allowed to leave Manchester United without being given a real chance to prove himself!

The one major disappointment for me about Mexico was the all too brief appearance of Bryan Robson on the world stage. His shoulder injury was a tragedy but it's in the past now, and that is good for England. Bryan's bravery in the box is marvellous to watch but it's been his downfall too. The man has a natural desire to go in where it hurts – marvellous for Manchester United and England, but it did cost us dearly in Mexico. Robson's fire might just have lit England in that fatal first hour against Argentina... instead all the aggression came that little bit too late.

And I have a thought for Bobby Robson as he plans the European campaign. Why not try Bryan Robson alongside Terry Butcher in the middle of defence? Butcher, as I've said, was outstanding in Mexico. With Robson alongside him, that dodgy England area through the middle at the back... might well be cemented... and a sound defence is the hall mark of a class side.

Robson's natural enthusiasm and drive would not be lost to England in that position. Forget about Butch Wilkins' indiscretion in Mexico. These things happen in the heat of World Cups. Keep Wilkins in so that Robson could move forward from a defensive role and Butch could plug the gap. That way we could have the best of both worlds from Bryan. Let's face it, every top team in Mexico had a central defender who could move out of defence with the ball and cause havoc. Remember Brown, Bossis, Caesar? Robson could be our ace in the hole. It's certainly worth thinking about.

Bryan still has to prove he is world class, but that will come I'm sure. As for Glenn Hoddle, the big Spurs man still has a way to go but I was pleased to see Bobby Robson give him his head in Mexico...

● *The boys who played Poland. Back row (left to right): Butcher, Lineker, Fenwick, Hoddle, G. Stevens, Shilton. Front row (left to right): Beardsley, Reid, Hodge, T. Stevens, Sansom*

for it worked. Glenn has outstanding talent and what all of the World's top stars possess... vision.

I know midfielders were given space in Mexico (some would say too much space) but Hoddle has the eye of a top rater. He can flight a ball to perfection and now that he has players like Lineker and Beardsley up front, with the same mental telepathy that all class players possess, he should be given a long run in the England team. Let's face it when the Brazilians and Argentinians suddenly take interest in 'Oddle of Inglaterra' you know the boy has what it takes.

As for Peter Shilton, well the man proved once again that he is amongst the top three goalkeepers in world football. I know how reassuring it is to any team to have a Shilton figure behind them. Gordon Banks gave us the same confidence in '66. And knowing Shilton he could well still be there come Italy 1990. He may be 36 now but that is young enough for a goalkeeper – just ask Pat Jennings!

I have one other plea to Bobby Robson: don't try to change our style! I know there will be those who, after Argentina's win will claim the South American route is the one we should take, but that is rubbish!

England's style is a natural up and at 'em method which again, if you think back to the Poland, Paraguay and Argentina matches, left the opposition breathless.

Of course the emphasis should be on ball control. The Brazilians seem to have some sort of super glue on their feet as they control the ball and that is to be envied. But there is nothing wrong with our style of play. We have players who can turn defence into attack quickly and their fitness was excellent in the rarefied atmosphere of Mexico.

Our next target is the European Championships and it would be stupid to try and change dramatically to the Brazilian blend on the sticky pitches we must endure in England during November to March. And now that we have the right players we should continue to exploit their natural aggression. No one in Europe (except perhaps the Scots!) will fancy facing England in full cry. That's for sure!

And one last thought. If the FA and Football League bosses really want to bask in England glory they should get off their backsides and completely change the League set-up. A First Division of sixteen clubs would give the players the chance they need to keep their legs fresh for international combat. Why not a fifth Division to achieve this? I don't reckon it would affect gates at a lower level but I do believe that less games would aid our European and world chances.

If I have gone on about England it is because I am delighted that at last we're on the right lines, but it should be mentioned that I enjoyed Scotland and Northern Ireland's attempts too.

The Saint no doubt will have plenty to say about Scotland but as an Englishman I felt Alex Ferguson's men didn't do too badly in the old Group of Death. All that was missing perhaps was a little more lucky white heather against the likes of Denmark and West Germany.

As for the Irish they didn't have the same success as in Spain but aren't they bonny fighters? Their comeback against the Spanish in Mexico had me on the edge of my seat and it is ironic to think that had they got the point they deserved they would have made the next round again.

But Billy Bingham did a magnificent job getting them to the finals and Billy can take some consolation in young Norman Whiteside, a natural leader of men. Still only 21 (I must check his birth certificate), his wholehearted aggression does not please everyone but I would not mind him in an England side! It is amazing to think that he could make not only Italy in 1990 but the 1994 World Cup as well.

And while I am on about the Irish, congratulations to my old mate Pat Jennings for bowing out so superbly at the top. He has blessed the game for 25 years. I knew him as a youngster at Spurs, as I've already mentioned, and I was throwing myself alongside him as he made those great saves against Brazil. I'd say he's earned his retirement. Mind you he's given Billy Bingham a problem. Where does he find a goalkeeper with a birth certificate which mentions a great great grandmother from Belfast?

MEXICO...FIRST TIME AROUND — *Saint*

So Greavsie fancies England are on song for another World Cup win. Fair enough but he should pray that Scotland aren't drawn against them in the qualifying series or, for that matter, anywhere in the tournament.

For despite being bitterly disappointed at Scotland not going through to the second round in Mexico, I did see enough to make me believe that winning the World Cup is not beyond Scotland either. As I keep reminding the bold Jim, one of these days England might pull a tough draw in qualifying matches and Scotland might pull an easy one. Then we might see some fireworks from the Scots.

I don't agree with Jimmy that it is easier to be in a tough group than a so-called easy one. I realise of course that nowadays even the so-called minnows can turn into sharks... just look at Morocco! But quite frankly both England and Scotland should take care of the Moroccos of world football and I believe that England's performance against them in Mexico should come under the same X-rating as Scotland's match with Iran in 1978.

OK so England came good against Poland in their final match while Scotland failed against the ten men of Uruguay, but even before the tournament, the Group of Death, as the Mexicans labelled the Scots' group, was always going to be the toughest of all. Yet there were signs of encouragement for the future.

We travelled 6000 miles and competed in every match. In the past we have been poor travellers and eight years ago I would not have put tuppence on Scotland's qualifying chances in such a group. Yet such was the preparation and attitude of caretaker boss Alex Ferguson and his backroom staff, that Scotland arrived in Mexico with no inferiority complex and ready to fight. That we didn't qualify is now World Cup history, but there was enough determination and skill in our performances against Denmark and West Germany to leave we Scots with that one quality we have in abundance where football is concerned... HOPE!

I was impressed with Scotland against Denmark. Alex Ferguson as usual had planned well and our first-half performance against Laudrup, Elkjaer and company was as good as I've ever seen from Scotland at such a high level of competition. But that old failing – lack of a top class striker – eventually did for us. As I watched on TV I couldn't help thinking back to my own days as a Scotland player and wishing that from somewhere we could unearth a young Denis Law. The Lawman I'm sure would have had the Danes dead and buried before they knew what hit them. As it was, the single goal defeat by the Danes was no disgrace for they were to my mind one of the teams of the tournament despite that strange 5–1 thrashing from Spain. Had Jesper Olsen of Manchester United not given away that silly penalty then Denmark might well have gone on to swamp Spain and win the tournament. As it was they established themselves as a team of quality... a team to savour perhaps in the European Championship Greavsie thinks may belong to England.

And the Scots can take hope in Denmark's success. Like Scotland their country has only five million inhabitants and, like the Scots, it is skill that counts when it comes to football.

Against West Germany too Scotland did well. When Gordon Strachan's goal beat Schumacher I felt we were on our way to a memorable victory but naivety crept in and in going for a second goal we gave the ever efficient Germans the chance to come back quickly, a chance they took in their usual clinical manner. Again though it was West Germany who were hanging on for dear life when the final whistle blew. Their 2–1 victory guaranteed them a second-round place but Scotland were pointless after two fine performances. Still, there was always Uruguay!

Uruguay went into the World Cup finals as one of the favourites. They left after a second-round defeat by Argentina with their reputation soiled for ever.

Following the bruising, bitter 0–0 draw with Scotland which earned them the match against

Maradona's Men, SFA secretary Ernie Walker, a man of the highest integrity, described them as 'the scum of world football, cheats and cowards. A disgrace.' He was right.

In the Neza dressing-rooms after the Scotland game the Uruguayans chanted 'We won the war'. They did of course, but they left a bad taste in the mouths of World Cup fans. Their constant hacking and time wasting may have got them the draw they needed but they won few friends, and only their own fans cried when they were put out by Argentina. The dirtiest team in the tournament were on their way home.

Having castigated Uruguay, I must say that Scotland's performance against Uruguay was diabolical. Never will my country have a better chance to progress. With the Uruguayans down to ten men after one minute when Baptista was ordered off for his vicious foul on Gordon Strachan, the door to the second round was ajar. That Scotland didn't burst it off its hinges was down to one of our most inept performances. In heat and altitude ten men should have no chance against eleven, yet, but for a feeble Steve Nichol shot, and a David Narey long-ranger I do not remember us looking likely to score.

Alex Ferguson took stick for completely re-shuffling his team after the Germany match. He dropped his skipper Graeme Souness and left out Maurice Malpas, bringing in Paul McStay and Arthur Albiston. Up front Steve Archibald got the chop in favour of Graham Sharp of Everton. Fergie's reason? He wanted to be as attack-minded as possible.

Ferguson took stick for his decisions, but I don't blame him. I blame the players for not succeeding. They were given the chance to put their country into the second stages of the World Cup and failed miserably.

Every one of Scotland's players against Uruguay was an experienced European campaigner. They must all have known that the first rule in Europe

● *The team which played against West Germany. Back row (left to right): Aitken, Leighton, S. Nichol, Narey, Gough, Miller. Front row (left to right): Souness, Malpas, Bannon, Strachan, Archibald*

when up against ten men is to keep possession. Run the opposition's guts out until finally they crack. Yet Scotland played like novices. Admittedly it was rough but we Scots have never been short on giving as good as we get and the best way to sicken the Uruguayans would have been to put a few into the back of their net. We were found lacking, possibly because of the nervousness which comes of realising you are within touching distance of the best result in your country's history. Nevertheless we failed.

The final whistle in that match was one of the most disappointing moments of my life. It was all there for the taking and we muffed it; and it showed on my face. Unbeknown to me millions were about to join me in my misery. For the backroom boys at London Weekend Television (who hosted the World Cup for ITV) had had a camera on me throughout and my reaction to every miss, every bad pass, every mistimed Scottish tackle had been recorded for posterity. I've watched it again – and it still makes pretty miserable viewing – I'm just surprised my language was so decent!

But now a few months later I realise that it is not beyond Scotland to win a World Cup. The late Jock Stein and Alex Ferguson have steadied Scotland. No one will hammer them as in the inconsistent old days.

I'm a believer in countries' soccer fortunes going in cycles. I was part of a fine Scottish side in the sixties. Willie Ormond's team of the seventies was excellent and right now we are not far short of being top class again.

We have a first-class goalkeeper in Jim Leighton. His Mexican performances proved that Greavsie's gags about Scottish goalkeepers are old hat, and Jim will still be around for Italy 1990. His Aberdeen team-mate and Scotland's new skipper Willie Miller was razor sharp in his reactions to danger in the Scots penalty box. Some of his tackling against West Germany and Denmark was amongst the best in the tournament. And in little Gordon Strachan we had a man who would fit easily into any Brazilian or Argentinian side. The little man's skills made him a

● *The star of Mexico '86: Diego Maradona*

major target for the World Cup destroyers, but they never quelled his spirit. He will be there for West Germany in 1988 and maybe even Italy two years later.

But it's time for our new manager to try the new boys up front. Of our front men in Mexico only Paul Sturrock and Charlie Nicholas passed muster. Frank McAvennie's first taste of the big time may do him good in years to come but we must look to the John Robertsons, the Gordon Duries, the Craig Leveins and Ally McCoists to show that they are World Cup material. For up front we are lacking. If Scotland can find the strikers then watch out Greavsie – England could be in trouble.

On a personal note, I found the whole World Cup thoroughly enjoyable. And while I would not advocate wholesale change of our style of play, there are things to be learned from Maradona, Platini, Caesar, Laudrup and company.

First we must play football on the ground. The traditional English style of play – long balls up the middle – is as dead as a Dodo. Cultured defenders deal easily with naive high balls and quickly turn defence into attack. One of my biggest regrets as a Scot was the non-appearance of Alan Hansen in the finals. Had he been there – and I'm sure Alex Ferguson now regrets his ommission – his ambling runs from defence would have given us an extra dimension similar to the top teams in the tournament, and who knows, that second round place might have been clinched. Every top team has a man capable of moving forward at speed from the back. We must develop that ploy too.

And we must be more adventurous up front. Too often our British teams allowed play to break down on the edge of the opposing penalty area because we were frightened to take a chance with those clever little 1–2s the French used to perfection, or those cunning flicks and hitch kicks so inherent in the Argentinian and Brazilian game. We must be more inventive up front. The Danes have introduced penalty box tricks to great effect. Why don't we?

Mexico disappointing? Anything but. Mind you, certain players I had hoped would command the world stage never quite managed to. Graeme Souness, Alain Giresse, Socrates, Frankie Vercautern and even Michel Platini in the later stages, all seemed to find the heat and the altitude just a little too much. Maradona didn't and that is why Argentina are World Champions.

They say that television is no substitute for the real thing and certainly there is nothing to beat the atmosphere of being at the World Cup finals but being a host with ITV in London did have its moments.

David Pleat, the new Tottenham manager, was a welcome addition to our ITV experts in Mexico and David had two classic bloopers. During England's 0–0 draw with Morocco he commented: 'There's a distinct lack of shooting in this match... that's something I'm looking forward to seeing more of!' And then this howler as Maradona got amongst the goals: 'He gets tremendous elevation with his balls no matter what position he's in!'

There were also those lively Brian Clough–Mike Channon confrontations. Cloughie at one point left Mike speechless (no easy matter) by saying, 'People are calling you the undertaker. You're always saying you want bodies in the box.'

Ron Atkinson of course featured highly in the ITV set-up and he caught me cold one night when, linking to Mexico, I asked him: 'Well, Ron, you've been with England all along... how do you think they're shaping up?'

I knew I was in trouble when that big grin spread over Ron's face and he answered: 'Don't have a clue Saint... I'm with the Irish not the English!' A little bit of Scotch egg on the face of yours truly.

Mind you we did get our own back on Big Ron. The big fellow always seemed to be glistening with oil and lounging suntanned round a pool every time we went over to Mexico. And after one confrontation he had with Gringo Greaves (alias Peter Brackley) we had a call from Greenpeace demanding that we throw him back into the water!

Peter Shilton and Trevor Francis made a couple of guest appearances and they almost broke Brian Moore's heart with two answers which had we panellists choking back the laughter. Brian asked Shilton, 'What do you know about Portugal, Peter?' Shilton replied, 'Well, Brian, I was there on my holidays a couple of years ago.'

Then there was the time when Mooro asked Francis what he thought about Peter Beardsley. 'Be quick, Trevor,' said Brian. 'We're running out of time.'

'I'll be quick,' replied Trevor. 'I've never seen him play!'

Maradona of course was everyone's man of the tournament. The little man was magical and to me justified everything I thought about him after seeing him play in the Ossie Ardiles testimonial game at White Hart Lane just a month before the finals. A brilliant footballer and modest with it.

Diego had the last word with Argentina in Mexico but Greavsie had the last word in telly terms when England met Argentina in the last eight. Jimmy had been warned by the guvnors not to mention the Falklands War but as usual the cracks came out: 'England must build an exclusion zone thirty-five yards out!'... 'We must send on some harriers!'... 'They tell me the Argies don't like subs.'

All very amusing. Mind you the Scots behind the scenes had the last word on that particular night. As the backroom boys were searching for some music for one of their popular musical montages the shout went up: 'Don't Cry for Me Argentina' or 'You Need Hands'.

The English were not amused!